Series/Number 07-115

D0661169

ANALYZING
REPEATED SURVEYS

GLENN FIREBAUGH
Pennsylvania State University

SAGE PUBLICATIONS
International Educatonal and Professional Publisher
Thousand Oaks   London   New Delhi

For information address:

 SAGE Publications, Inc.
2455 Teller Road
Thousand Oaks, California 91320
E-mail: order@sagepub.com

SAGE Publications Ltd.
6 Bonhill Street
London EC2A 4PU
United Kingdom

SAGE Publications India Pvt. Ltd.
M-32 Market
Greater Kailash I
New Delhi 110 048 India

Printed in the United States of America

Library of Congress Cataloging-in-Publication Data

Firebaugh, Glenn.
    Analyzing repeated surveys / author, Glenn Firebaugh.
      p. cm.—(Quantitative applications in the social sciences; v. 115)
    ISBN 0-8039-7398-5 (pbk.: acid-free paper)
    1. Social surveys. 2. Social surveys—Methodology. 3. Change
(Psychology) I. Title. II. Series: Sage university papers series.
Quantitative applications in the social sciences; v. 115.
HN29.F54 1997
300'.723—dc20   96-35622

06 07 08 09 10   10 9 8 7 6 5 4

Acquiring Editor:	C. Deborah Laughton
Editorial Assistant:	Eileen Carr
Production Editor:	Diana E. Axelsen
Production Assistant:	Denise Santoyo
Typesetter/Designer:	Andrea Swanson/Dick Palmer

When citing a university paper, please use the proper form. Remember to cite the Sage University Paper series title and include the paper number. One of the following formats can be adapted (depending on the style manual used):

(1) Jaccard, J., & Wan, C. K. (1996). *LISREL approaches to interaction effects in multiple regression* (Sage University Paper series on Quantitative Applications in the Social Sciences, No. 07-114). Thousand Oaks, CA: Sage.

OR

(2) Jaccard, J., & Wan, C. K. 1996. *LISREL approaches to interaction effects in multiple regression.* Sage University Paper series on Quantitative Applications in the Social Sciences, series no. 07-114. Thousand Oaks, CA: Sage.

CONTENTS

SERIES EDITOR'S INTRODUCTION

Survey research is a boom enterprise, and our series has fostered that work through several papers (Kalton, No. 35; Converse & Presser, No. 63; Lee, Forthofer, & Lorimor, No. 71; Saris, No. 80; and Bourque & Clark, No. 85). Those worthwhile expositions essentially assume, as does the rest of the relevant literature, that the investigator wishes to conduct a single survey. Thousands have been so conducted. We now observe, at century's end, that many "single" surveys actually have been repeated a number of times. Repeated surveys, in Professor Firebaugh's words, "ask the same questions to different samples." Well-known examples include the General Social Survey, the National Election Study, and the National Health Interview Survey. For some time, these surveys have regularly administered the same set of items to newly selected national samples. To illustrate, the National Election Study has fielded an extensive battery of questions on political attitudes and behavior in every congressional and presidential election since its beginning in 1952.

Such repeated surveys present researchers with a growing opportunity to analyze changes in society as a whole. They allow a shift of focus, from an investigation of individual-level microprocesses to one of aggregate-level macroprocesses. Firebaugh explicates different methods for studying social change in this way. To provide a general theoretical orientation, he first wrestles with the classic issue of how to separate cohort, period, and age effects. Imagine that one records an increase in pro-war attitudes among former Vietnam War protesters. Why might this be so? Is there a period effect, such as a general rise in society's war tolerance? Or is there an age effect, such as that aging brings on a greater acceptance of war? Or is there a cohort effect, such as that the pro-war attitudes of those born after 1950 are higher? These three kinds of effects are difficult to sort out because of the identification problem. Strategies for overcoming this problem, in the context of careful attention to theory, are insightfully discussed.

Surveys that have been repeated often enough permit the meaningful study of aggregate trends. For example, supposing that pro-war attitudes of the public are measured the same way over a series of surveys, the change analyst may plot that trend. In addition, a comparison of different groups within the society could be made, for example, former Vietnam War protesters compared to nonprotesters. Firebaugh shows how to estimate group differences in trends and illustrates the process in a convincing exploration, using real data, of the gap between young and old Americans on social spending attitudes. The aggregate trends themselves can be broken down, with the overall change attributed either to individuals or to population groups. This is called "proximate decomposition," carried out by either regression or algebra. As an example, the trend in antiblack prejudice from 1972 to 1984 is decomposed, revealing that the overall change comes a bit more from cohort replacement than from individual change.

Aggregate change may be the object of explanatory, rather than descriptive, decomposition. Using a regression format, aggregate change divides into causal components from an intercept change, the change in the levels of the independent variables, and the change in the slope of the independent variables. To display this more general decomposition strategy, Firebaugh explains trends in U.S. voting turnout, accompanying the explanation with a healthy cautionary note against mere mechanical application of the method.

In contrast to the study of aggregate change, the penultimate chapter examines repeated surveys through changing-parameter models, where over time the impact of an independent variable X on a dependent variable Y changes at the individual level. Repeated surveys are pooled, or cumulated, into one data set for analysis. Well-chosen examples from U.S. election survey data examine the changing impact of key party identification determinants, such as region, education, race, and class.

Altogether, the monograph develops four basic uses of repeated surveys: description, decomposition, and explanation of aggregate trends, plus assessment of changing individual parameters. Systematic exploitation of repeated surveys greatly extends possibilities for analysis of change. Firebaugh's clearly written, unique compilation is an invaluable guide to this emergent research area.

—Michael S. Lewis-Beck
Series Editor

PREFACE

Were the title not so cumbersome, I would have called this monograph *How to Use Repeated Surveys to Analyze Social Change.* This is a "how to" book, with the focus on simple but useful methods for exploiting the repetition in repeated surveys.

Because the study of social change is a central enterprise in all the social sciences, I have tried to make the text accessible to a very wide audience. I assume only that the reader understands the fundamentals of regression analysis.

The monograph is based on a short summer course I have taught the past few years at the University of Michigan's Institute for Social Research (ISR). I wish to thank Duane Alwin, former Director of the Summer Institute at ISR, for his invitation to teach the course; Michael Hughes, Virginia Tech, for his suggestion that I transcribe the lecture notes into a book for the Sage series on Quantitative Applications in the Social Sciences; Scott Menard, University of Colorado, Charles W. Mueller, University of Iowa, and Helmut Norpoth, State University of New York at Stony Brook, for reviewing the manuscript; and the students in the courses for their refusal to accept muddled exposition.

To Judy Rae, with love and gratitude.

ANALYZING REPEATED SURVEYS

GLENN FIREBAUGH
Pennsylvania State University

1. INTRODUCTION

Repeated Surveys: Same Questions, Different Samples

Repeated surveys ask the same questions to different samples of people. Because a new sample is selected at each measurement period, another name for the repeated survey design is "repeated cross-sectional design" (Menard, 1991). Some surveys are repeated at a fixed interval (usually monthly, quarterly, annually, or biennially); Duncan and Kalton (1987) call these "periodic surveys." Other surveys, such as polls before impending elections, are repeated on an occasional basis. With regard to social change—the focus of this book—periodic surveys are the easiest to analyze.

In distinguishing a repeated survey design (different samples over time) from a panel survey design (reinterviews of the same individuals), it is important to keep in mind that the terms "panel" and "repeated survey" refer to the essence of the sample design. Some panel studies regularly add individuals to the sample, and some repeated surveys contain a panel component, so the term "repeated survey" does not necessarily imply entirely new samples for each survey. It is usually easier and cheaper to reinterview earlier respondents than it is to select and interview new respondents, especially in cases in which reinterviews can be done by telephone; moreover, reinterviews enable the study of change in individuals over time, because specific individuals can be followed.

Nationwide repeated surveys have become a staple of American social science research over the past quarter century. Probably the best known of such repeated surveys is the General Social Survey or GSS, an annual (biennial, beginning in 1994) personal interview survey of the noninstitutionalized adult population of the contiguous 48 states. Since the first survey in 1972, more than 32,000 respondents have answered about 1,500 different questions covering a wide variety of attitudes, beliefs, and behaviors. The data thus assembled have become a national resource for the

1

social sciences. Over the past two decades, the GSS no doubt has become the most heavily used data source in the social sciences outside data from the U.S. Census. The 10th edition of the *Annotated Bibliography of Papers Using the General Social Surveys* (Smith, Arnold, & Wesely, 1995) lists about 3,000 scholarly papers based in whole or in part on GSS data. In addition, the GSS is used heavily for pedagogical purposes. Software packages have been developed specifically to teach sociology using the GSS, and it is estimated that each year more than 100,000 sociology students utilize the GSS in some form in their classes.

Although the GSS is the "only U.S. survey that guarantees replication of questions" (Davis & Smith, 1992, p. 1), other periodic nationwide surveys also contain substantial repetition from survey to survey. These include the National Election Study (NES), which has usable biennial data from 1952; the National Health Interview Survey (NHIS), an annual data collection begun in 1957; and the Current Population Survey (CPS), a monthly survey of labor force activity based on a rotating panel design. In addition, occasional polls—such as the CBS/New York Times polls—often repeat items. Other important data sets with replicated items include the Consumer Surveys (University of Michigan's Survey Research Center), which provide data on some questions as far back as 1946. These data sets are available through the Inter-University Consortium for Political and Social Research (ICPSR), housed at the University of Michigan. Interested readers should consult the most recent ICPSR catalog and Kiecolt and Nathan (1985) for further description of national surveys useful for the study of social change.

Repeated Surveys Versus Panel Surveys

To study change, we must measure the same thing at different points in time. Repeated surveys administer the measures to different people. Panel surveys repeatedly measure the same people. Panel surveys thus follow individuals over time, whereas repeated surveys follow birth cohorts (people born the same year) over time.

Which method is better? There is no general answer, because panel data are better suited to address some issues and repeated cross sections are better for other issues (Duncan & Kalton, 1987). Suppose we want to know whether the ratio of Republicans to Democrats increased in the voting-age population during the Reagan presidency. Estimation of the ratio is straightforward with repeated surveys of the population. Using NES data (Abramson, Aldrich, and Rohde, 1994, Table 8-1), for example, we estimate that the ratio increased from 0.55 in 1980 (of party partisans, 35.4% are Republicans, 64.6% are Democrats) to 0.78 in 1988 (43.8% Republicans, 56.3% Democrats). This increase is noteworthy, if only because it suggests that Republican candidates tended to begin with a broader base of support in the late 1980s than they did in the early 1980s.

Note, however, that trends in percentage Republican and percentage Democrat do not tell us about the volume of party switching that occurred during the Reagan presidency. At one extreme, suppose that *no one* switched parties, so that any observed increase in the ratio of Republicans to Democrats would be due entirely to cohort replacement (the replacement of older, more Democratic birth cohorts with younger, more Republican ones). In this instance, the trend gives an inflated impression of the rate of party switching, which was zero. It is more likely, though, that the trend in the ratio of Republicans to Democrats understates (not overstates) the rate of party switching, because people switch parties both ways, and such offsetting movement is not captured by the aggregate ratio.

Because repeated surveys do not follow individuals over time, they do not capture "gross change" in party affiliation; that is, repeated surveys do not capture the actual rate of party switching among individuals. Repeated surveys instead capture "net change"— the *net effect* of all the changes.

Because panel surveys follow individuals over time, they provide estimates of both gross and net change *within birth cohorts*. The reliability of panel estimates of gross change depends on the rapidity of the change relative to the measurement interval. Most party switching likely would be detected with annual measurement, because people generally do not switch parties several times a year. Other political phenomena are more fickle, however. For example, people might change their minds pretty often regarding how well they think the incumbent president is doing; with regard to the president's popularity, then, gross individual change is likely to be understated when measured on an annual basis.

For our purposes here, the more important point is that the traditional panel design is ill-suited to estimate *net change* for the *overall population*. In the traditional panel design, individuals are selected at time 1 and followed up; hence, in this design, new birth cohorts are not added over time. As a result, we cannot estimate net change for the overall population. For example, with the traditional panel survey design, we could not determine whether or not the ratio of Republicans to Democrats increased in the voting-age population during the Reagan presidency.

Neither research design, therefore, is a panacea. Repeated surveys are ill-suited for estimating gross change among individuals, whereas traditional panel surveys are ill-suited for estimating aggregate trends. To overcome these limitations, survey methodologists have developed designs combining the features of both panels and repeated cross sections. One such hybrid is the "rotating panel survey" (Duncan & Kalton, 1987). In rotating panel surveys, panels are rotated—new panels added, old ones rotated off—to maintain up-to-date samples of changing populations. The CPS and the Survey on Income and Program Participation (SIPP) are examples of rotating panel surveys. A second hybrid, the "split panel survey" (Duncan & Kalton, 1987), solves the problem of estimating gross change in repeated surveys by adding a panel component to repeated surveys. The British Social Attitudes Survey is an example of a split panel survey. The NES is partially a split panel survey, because it includes panel components for selected surveys (Kiecolt & Nathan, 1985).

Kish (1983, 1986) recommends the use of split panel designs, and split designs and other hybrids likely will become more common in the future. Nevertheless, extant survey data sets commonly are either repeated cross sections (with no panel component) or panels. Panel data are treated in two previous books in this series (Finkel, 1995; Markus, 1979). Our concern here is the analysis of repeated surveys, including split panel and other survey designs that have a substantial repeated survey component.

Analytic Designs for Repeated Surveys

There are at least three basic approaches to analyzing repeated surveys. One possibility is simply to analyze the surveys separately. In this approach, analyzing repeated surveys is the same as analyzing a single survey, except that the procedures are repeated for several surveys. I can think of no compelling reason for doing this (except perhaps at the exploratory stage of an analysis, as a preliminary check on whether the effects of the explanatory variables appear to have changed over time). If the objective is to estimate individual-level relationships at a particular point in time, then the analysis of a single survey suffices. If the objective is to determine whether or not a relationship has changed, then to test for statistical significance, it is easier to cumulate or "pool" the surveys than to analyze them separately (see Chapter 6). Even if effects have remained constant, it is better to pool the data, because pooling would provide more precise estimates of the (constant) effects.[1] In short, if one's interest is in social change, I see little reason to analyze repeated surveys separately, so I do not promote that strategy in this book.

A second possibility is to use the cumulated cross sections to analyze the size and stability of individual-level relationships. For example, researchers could use this approach to determine if the relationship between class and political party affiliation has remained stable over time. Very often, the cumulated-data approach does not involve any special effort in data setup, because heavily used repeated surveys such as the GSS and the NES can be purchased in this form. The cumulated-surveys approach is a flexible one, providing the researcher with the basis for testing for change in individual-level or "micro" relationships over time. Chapter 5 presents a general decomposition model that clarifies how microlevel change contributes to aggregate change. Chapter 6 describes and illustrates simple models for cumulated data that can be used to test for microlevel change, that is, for change in individual-level relationships.

A third possibility is to use the cumulated surveys to analyze aggregate change. A special feature of this book is its emphasis on the analysis of change at the macro level. Chapter 3 describes and illustrates methods for estimating aggregate trends. Chapter 4 describes how to decompose trends into (a) the part resulting from net change within birth cohorts and (b) the part resulting from cohort replacement (that is, the effect of population turnover). Because the cohort analytic framework is fundamental to our discussion of aggregate trends, Chapter 2 reviews cohort analysis and describes methods for disentangling cohort effects, age effects, and period effects.

A Note on Terminology

Because the meaning of terms such as "decomposition" can vary from discipline to discipline, in this book I try to minimize confusion by providing equations that formalize the concepts and by providing examples to illustrate the equations. The term "pooled data" is a good example of how terms can be ambiguous. In this chapter, I have referred several times to combining or "pooling" surveys. Although that terminology is used in the survey literature, one must be careful not to confuse pooled data in the sense of combined surveys with pooled data as used by econometricians to refer to combined time-series/cross-sectional data (see Sayrs, 1989), that is, panel data. Thus, in econometrics, there is a literature on the use of unit-specific terms in "pooled data" to control for enduring traits of individual units that affect Y but are hard to measure (for example, a person's drive to succeed, or a nation's topography, when the units are nations). Obviously, we cannot control for such unit-specific traits unless we have multiple measurements for a given individual—and we do *not* get this from pooling repeated surveys. "Pooled data," therefore, sometimes means the same individual units followed over time and sometimes means different samples at different points in time. To avoid confusion below, I use the term "cumulated data" to refer to repeated surveys that have been combined.

2. DISTINGUISHING AGE, PERIOD, AND COHORT EFFECTS

By attempting to distinguish the effects of birth cohort, of aging, and of historical period, cohort analysis provides a template for thinking about social change. I rely on that template in this book, especially in the discussion of aggregate change (Chapters 3 and 4). Because those chapters borrow heavily from fundamental concepts of cohort analysis, in this chapter I briefly review those concepts. I begin by defining cohort effects and distinguishing them from age effects and period effects. Then I describe different approaches to the thorny problem of how to separate cohort, period, and age effects empirically. Readers already familiar with cohort analysis can go directly to the discussion of how to disentangle age, period, and cohort effects.

Age, Period, and Cohort Effects

Social scientists often use cohort analysis as their point of departure in the study of change. Suppose we observe that church attendance has risen among a group of adults we have studied since they were adolescents. How are we to account for that increase? A cohort analyst will immediately think in terms of two types of processes. The increase could be due to general events or processes associated with the historical era; perhaps there is a general revival of interest in religion during the era studied (*period effect*). Alternatively, the increase might result from more specific processes related to aging or life-cycle status (*age effect*); as young adults settle down in a community, marry, have children, and so on, they are more likely to attend church—just as their parents did, and their grandparents before that. In other words, the cohorts under study are merely replicating the church attendance trajectories of prior generations.

It is possible, of course, that the increasing church attendance over time reflects a combination of age and period effects. Perhaps life-cycle and revival effects combine to produce the within-cohort increase, or perhaps life-cycle effects operate to boost attendance whereas secularization (a period effect) works to depress attendance, and the observed increase reflects the net effect of the countervailing forces (in this case, the stronger effect of life-cycle status).

Now consider the case in which we observe age differences at a given point in time, as opposed to change as cohorts age over time. For example, we might observe that those in their 20s are less likely than others to vote in presidential elections. Again, a cohort analyst will immediately think of two categories of explanation. One is the age or life-cycle explanation: The young tend to be less established in a community, they are more likely to be in school, they might have young children to care for, and so on. If age effects account for the depressed voting of the young, we can expect successive cohorts to reproduce the life-cycle voting pattern of their predecessors, with low rates at first followed by higher rates of voting as the cohorts reach middle age. Alternatively, the new cohorts might exhibit depressed voting rates throughout their life spans, suggesting a *cohort effect* rather than an age effect. In this case, the younger cohorts are different not because they are younger, but because they were *born at a different time*. As Ryder (1965, p. 844) puts it, cohort effects come about because "members of any cohort are entitled to participate in only one slice of life—their unique location in the stream of history."

In short, "cohort effect" refers to cohort differences that result from the common experiences or reactions of a cohort, "age effect" refers to change produced by influences associated with age, and "period effect" refers to change produced by influences associated with the historical era. Cohort effects arise from the unique experiences and socialization of cohorts as well as from the unique reactions of cohorts to the *same* historical events (the young, for example, might be more profoundly affected by watershed events, such as the assassination of President Kennedy or the Iran hostage affair).[2] Age effects can be based on "wired in" developmental or maturational changes or on physiological changes related to aging, as well as on life-cycle statuses (marital status, parental status) that are related to age. Period effects refer to the uniform effects of the historical context, that is, to events or historical conditions that affect all cohorts uniformly. (See Glenn, 1977, and Hagenaars, 1990, for further discussion of age, period, and cohort effects.)

The Identification Problem

Attempts to separate age, period, and cohort effects are bedeviled by the identity given in this equation:

$$\text{Year of birth} = \text{Year of measurement} - \text{Age}. \qquad (2.1)$$

Equation 2.1 states that year of birth, or cohort, is a linear function of year of measurement (period) and age. Thus, if we were to enter all three variables—cohort (year of birth), period (year of measurement), and age— as regressors in a regression model, we could not estimate the model. That is, we cannot estimate this model:

$$E(Y) = \beta_0 + \beta_P Period + \beta_A Age + \beta_C Cohort \qquad (2.2)$$

where $E(Y)$ is the expected value of Y, *Period* is year of measurement, *Age* is in years, and *Cohort* is year of birth. (Here, and throughout the monograph, I use Greek letters to denote population parameters; so β denotes population parameter, *not* standardized slope.)

To better understand why there is an estimation problem, consider the interpretation of β_C in Equation 2.2. β_C is the expected change in Y when birth year is increased one year, *holding constant* year of measurement and age. When age and year are fixed, however, birth year cannot change, because birth year = year – age. Similarly, the period slope β_P cannot be estimated for fixed age and cohort, and the age slope β_A cannot be estimated for fixed period and cohort. This is the identification problem in cohort analysis.

Two specious solutions to the problem are easily dispensed with at the outset. Regressing Y on all three combinations of the pairs—age and period, age and cohort, and period and cohort —is not informative. Because age and period contains the same information as age and cohort or period and cohort, we will get the same R^2 for each of the models, so we cannot use "best fit" as a criterion for determining the proper model here. Nor does it help to perform a cross-sectional analysis to eliminate the possibility of period effects. By doing cross-sectional analysis, we substitute a constant, k, for year of measurement in Equation 2.1, yielding cohort = k – age; hence, we still cannot distinguish a cohort effect from an age effect. The problem of disentangling cohort and age effects therefore is not solved by the use of cross-sectional analysis.

Strategies for Overcoming the Identification Problem

There is no foolproof technical trick for disentangling age, period, and cohort effects (Wilmoth, 1990). There are, however, defensible strategies for addressing the identification problem. To be convincing, cohort analyses often employ one or more of the following strategies (Firebaugh & Chen, 1995).

Fixing Coefficients A Priori. One common strategy is to make identifying assumptions. In one version of this strategy, researchers assume that one of the effects—age, period, or cohort—is zero, or at least is small enough to be safely ignored. For example, if we assume that age effects can be safely ignored, then we fix $\beta_A = 0$ in Equation 2.2 and simply regress Y on period and cohort.

The problem with this strategy is that the results are only as reliable as the identifying assumption that $\beta_A = 0$. If that assumption is wrong, then our estimates of period effects and cohort effects will be contaminated by age effects. This is easy to see by substituting Age = Period – Cohort into Equation 2.2:

$$E(Y) = \beta_0 + \beta_P Period + \beta_A Age + \beta_C Cohort \text{ [not estimable]}$$

$$= \beta_0 + \beta_P Period + \beta_A (Period - Cohort) + \beta_C Cohort$$

$$= \beta_0 + (\beta_P + \beta_A) Period + (\beta_C - \beta_A) Cohort. \qquad (2.3)$$

In other words, getting estimates is not a problem when we regress Y on period and cohort; we will in fact get a coefficient for the period term and a coefficient for the cohort term. The problem is in *interpreting* the two coefficients. As Equation 2.3 demonstrates, the period coefficient is the sum of the period effect and the age effect, $\beta_P + \beta_A$, whereas the cohort coefficient is the difference between the cohort effect and the age effect, $\beta_C - \beta_A$. Hence, the slopes in Equation 2.3 yield unbiased estimates of period and cohort effects only if the age effect is in fact zero; otherwise, the coefficient for period reflects age as well as period effects, and the coefficient for cohort reflects age as well as cohort effects.

Other identifying assumptions could be made. For example, Mason, Mason, Winsborough, and Poole (1973) show that estimates of age, period, and cohort effects in categorical data analysis can be obtained by constraining selected adjacent cohorts (or ages, or periods) to be the same. Although assuming constant effects for adjacent categories generally is more prudent than simply assuming away one of the effects, even the assumption of constant effects for adjacent categories can be wrong, leading to unreliable results (Glenn, 1976). Moreover, a large sample is required for stable estimates because of the high levels of collinearity among the age, period, and cohort terms. By constraining adjacent categories to have the same effects, we can get estimates, because period, cohort, and age no longer are perfectly collinear. Although they no longer are perfectly collinear, however, there is nevertheless a high degree of collinearity among the three variables (the correlation of any two, with the third controlled, will approximate 1.0). Estimates of period, cohort, and age effects therefore are likely to be unstable, especially in small samples.

Using Side Information. When we refer to the age-period-cohort identification problem, we are referring to the fact that an observed pattern of results can be accounted for, mathematically, by more than one combination of age, period, and cohort effects. Typically, however, the mathematical possibilities are not all equally plausible substantively. "Side information" refers to knowledge that enables one to judge the relative plausibility of alternative interpretations of observed results (Glenn, 1977). The existence of nonlinear relationships involving one or more of the three predictors (age, period, and cohort) provides leverage in this regard, because there often is only one plausible explanation for a particular nonlinear pattern (for example, an inverted-U pattern for earnings and age is almost certainly an age—not cohort—effect on earnings).

Consider Equation 2.4, in which the regressors are age and period:

$$E(Y) = \beta_0 + \beta_A Age + \beta_C Cohort + \beta_P Period \text{ [not estimable]}$$

$$= \beta_0 + \beta_A Age + \beta_C (Period - Age) + \beta_P Period$$

$$= \beta_0 + (\beta_A - \beta_C) Age + (\beta_P + \beta_C) Period. \tag{2.4}$$

Let Y = annual church attendance (number of times an adult attends per year), and suppose we obtain $E(Attend) = 5 + 0.5(Age)$ when we regress attendance on period and age. The positive coefficient for age indicates that older adults are more likely to attend church. The zero coefficient for period indicates that age-specific church rates are constant over time; that is, at a given age, successive cohorts attend church at the same rate. The pattern, then, is one of increasing church attendance over the life cycle, with successive cohorts repeating the attendance patterns of their predecessors. Mathematically, this pattern could arise from various combinations of age, period, and cohort effects; for example, $\beta_C = -0.5$ and $\beta_P = 0.5$ (negative cohort effects exactly offset by positive period effects, so $\beta_P + \beta_C = 0$) and no age effect ($\beta_A = 0$), so $\beta_A - \beta_C = 0.5$. That combination is farfetched, however. It is much more likely that the pattern of coincident cohort attendance trajectories reflects a pure age effect, $\beta_A = 0.5$ (Firebaugh & Harley, 1991). In any case, the point is that some mathematical possibilities are more likely than others, and that fact can provide leverage in disentangling age, period, and cohort effects (Glenn, 1976, 1977).

Using Direct Measurement. The direct measurement strategy is commonly used when cohort differences are hypothesized to originate from the cohorts' relative *sizes* (Easterlin, 1980). In such instances, the telling feature of the cohort (its size) is easy to measure. In most other instances, the telling feature is less clear-cut and much more difficult to measure. Consider, for example, the sorts of cohort effects discussed by Ryder (1965), effects resulting from the greater impact of "social transformations" on the young (p. 861). Although it is commonly assumed that the young are in fact more impressionable (Glenn, 1980; Mannheim, 1927/1952), identifying and measuring the social transformations that produce lasting cohort differences is a daunting task. Likewise, it is often a daunting task to measure the social transformations that produce period effects and to measure the age-related influences that produce age effects. The task is difficult in part because it is hard to prove that one's direct measures are exhaustive. For example, if key life-cycle statuses (marital status, parental status, work status, and so on) are used to measure an age effect, then critics can always argue that such statuses capture only a fraction of the bundle of age-based influences referenced by the term "age effect."

In short, there is no "magic bullet" for separating age, period, and cohort effects, but there are strategies for dealing with the identification problem. Common to each strategy is the need for careful theorizing about the nature of age, period, and cohort effects. The importance of theory is transparent in the case of the "side information" and direct measurement strategies. Theory is no less important in the "technical fix" strategy, in which identifying constraints are applied to the model a priori. The identifying constraints must be based on careful theorizing, because incorrect assumptions will yield unreliable results. When plausible alternative identifying assumptions are available, it is prudent to test the sensitivity of results to the identifying assumptions by comparing the estimates of age, period, and cohort effects under those alternative identifying assumptions.

3. AGGREGATE TRENDS

Many repeated survey data sets now span several decades, and it is possible to detect social trends. The trick is to distinguish trends from erratic fluctuations.

Smoothing Trends

Change in Y, time 1 to time 2, is defined as $Y_2 - Y_1$. Analyses of repeated surveys sometimes overinterpret this difference, especially for short time intervals. An observed difference from one survey to another is sometimes used as the basis for a claim that society is moving in one direction or another. One should be wary of such claims. Because of sampling error and erratic short-term fluctuations, relying on measurements at two points in time to intuit social trends is imprudent.

Many repeated surveys have cumulated a decade or more of annual or biennial data, and such surveys provide a firmer basis for conclusions regarding social trends. The basic analytic principle that more data is better than less data applies to the analysis of social trends. Often it will not do merely to examine the difference between the end points; we want to use all the surveys. The question then is how to smooth the survey-to-survey fluctuations in the data to determine if there is an underlying trend.

One option is to use moving averages. Consider the aggregate time series $Y_1, Y_2, \ldots, Y_T$, where the Ys are simple averages for years $1, 2, \ldots, T$. The moving average for Y at time t is determined by using a weighted average of Y values adjacent to Y_t as well as Y_t itself. In a 5-year moving average, for example, the moving average for Y at time t is the weighted average of $\{Y_{t-2}, Y_{t-1}, Y_t, Y_{t+1}, Y_{t+2}\}$, where the weights can be $\{1/9, 2/9, 3/9, 2/9, 1/9\}$, respectively. (See Kendall, 1973, p. 35 for derivation of the weights. This weighting gives more emphasis to more current values. Another possible weighting is 1/5 for each term, giving equal emphasis to each.) Weighted averages are a useful first step, if only to produce a graph that smooths out sampling fluctuation. The smoothed graph may help in determining whether change in Y reverses direction over the interval—in which case it would be misleading to fit a linear trend to the data.

If it is appropriate to fit a linear trend, regression can be used to determine whether the sample trend is statistically significant. Suppose there are T annual repeated surveys. A logical step is to regress Y_{it} on year of survey:

$$E(Y_{it}) = \beta_0 + \beta_1 Year_{it} \qquad (3.1)$$

$$\text{where: } i = 1, 2, \ldots, I_t; \, t = 1, 2, \ldots, T. \qquad (3.2)$$

E(Y) is the expected value of *Y*, Y_{it} denotes *Y* for the ith person in the tth survey, and I_t denotes sample size of the tth survey. Here, $E(Y_{it})$ is a *conditional* mean (the expected value or mean of *Y* is expressed as a function of year). A nonzero β_1 implies that the mean of *Y* is a linear function of year. The sign of the slope indicates whether *Y* is trending upward or downward. In estimating Equation 3.1, it is convenient to code *Year* = 0 for $t = 1$ (the first survey year); then β_0 is the predicted *Y*-mean for the initial year of the study.

It is common for surveys to oversample certain groups. In some cases, the oversampling is intentional (to ensure sufficient minority members in the sample). In other cases, the oversampling is a byproduct of the sample design; for example, by selecting households and interviewing only one individual in the household, some surveys oversample adults who live alone. In such instances, weights can be used to restore the correct population proportions (Stephenson, 1978). The basic rule of sample weighting is to use weights that are inversely proportional to the selection probability (Kalton, 1983). Consider, for example, a target population with two groups— *M* (majority) and *m* (minority) that comprise 90% and 10% of the population, respectively. To ensure sufficient minority members in the sample, suppose the sample proportions are .20 for *m* and .80 for *M*. To restore the correct population proportions, we weight members of *m* by .10/.20 = 0.5 and members of *M* by .90/.80 = 1.125.[3]

Finally, it should be underscored that the use of Equation 3.1 to detect trends assumes that the items being compared are equivalent from survey to survey (Smith, 1993). "House effects" (Johnston, 1981) constitute one threat to equivalence, so for trend analysis it is best when the data come from a single survey organization. In instances in which that is not possible, a historical trend sometimes can be constructed by splicing data from two survey organizations that have asked the same question at different points in time. Splicing assumes that the two historical series overlap in time. If the series are simply joined (no overlap) as opposed to spliced, at the point of connection of the two series it is hard to distinguish real change from change resulting from house effects.

Data from a single survey firm is no panacea, however. Experienced survey researchers know that sometimes even a seemingly innocuous change in wording of a question can produce a significant change in responses (Rasinski, 1988; Smith, 1987). Moreover, responses to a particular question in a survey can be affected by the nature of the other questions in the survey, so even if question Q remains constant from survey to survey, changes in *other* questions in the survey might produce changes in response to Q because of "context effects" (Smith, 1988, 1991). Even when wording and context are equivalent from survey to survey, there remains the possibility that the meaning of key words (such as "conservative" and "liberal") has changed over time. In determining *why* there is a trend in repeated surveys, one should first ask whether the trend merely reflects changes in the way respondents are *interpreting* the survey item.

Group Differences in Trends: Convergence and Divergence

The direction of an overall trend might mask differences in trends for key groups within a society. For example, surveys indicate that opposition to marriage between blacks and whites has declined in recent decades in the United States (Firebaugh & Davis, 1988; Gallup & Newport, 1991). That overall trend could mask important regional or group differences. Has the decline been faster or slower in the South? Has opposition declined at the same rate for men and women, and for blacks and whites? Have the trends crossed for white women and black women, so that now black women are more likely than white women to oppose interracial marriages (Paset & Taylor, 1991)?

There are five possibilities regarding group differences in linear trends: coincident trends, parallel trends, converging trends, diverging trends, and crossed trends. Suppose, for example, that we estimated trends in whites' opposition to interracial marriage separately for the South (S) and the Nonsouth (N). Separate estimates could be obtained by using separate regression equations:

$$E(Y_{it}^{S}) = \beta_0^S + \beta_1^S Year_{it} \tag{3.3}$$

$$E(Y_{it}^{N}) = \beta_0^N + \beta_1^N Year_{it} \tag{3.4}$$

where Y is opposition to interracial marriage and, as before, i indexes individual and t indexes survey. Equation 3.3 yields the linear trend for the South and Equation 3.4 yields the linear trend for the Nonsouth. If we set $Year = 0$ for the first survey, then the intercepts are estimates[4]—for the South and Nonsouth respectively—of opposition to interracial marriage at the beginning of the study. To simplify the notation, I assume here that the measurement interval is in years, but the measurement could be quarterly, monthly, or at other intervals. In that case, we would alter the regressor accordingly; for example, $Quarter_{it}$ or $Month_{it}$ would replace $Year_{it}$ in Equations 3.3 and 3.4.

Instead of estimating separate regression equations for the South and Nonsouth, it is often more convenient to combine the equations into a single equation. Equations 3.3 and 3.4 can be combined using a dummy variable and an interaction term:

$$E(Y_{it}) = \beta_0^* + \beta_1^* Year_{it} + \delta_0 S_{it} + \delta_1 [S \times Year]_{it} \qquad (3.5)$$

where S is a dummy variable coded $1 =$ South. The single equation method offers this key advantage: Because δ_0 and δ_1 in Equation 3.5 represent differences in intercepts and slopes, respectively, we can determine immediately whether or not there are initial differences (δ_0) and trend differences (δ_1) between the South and Nonsouth.

If δ_0 and δ_1 are both zero, then the trends are coincident for the South and Nonsouth (same intercepts and same slopes). If δ_0 is nonzero and δ_1 is zero, the trends are parallel. If δ_0 and δ_1 are nonzero and have the same sign, the trends are divergent. If δ_0 and δ_1 are nonzero and have opposing signs, the trends are convergent (or, perhaps, have crossed, depending on the initial difference between the South and Nonsouth, and the rate of convergence).

The foregoing principles are easy to derive. Substituting 0 for the Nonsouth in Equation 3.5, we get

$$E(Y_{it}) = \beta_0^* + \beta_1^* Year_{it}. \qquad (3.6)$$

Clearly, then, $\beta_0^* = \beta_0^N$ (intercept for the Nonsouth) and $\beta_1^* = \beta_1^N$ (slope for the Nonsouth). Substituting 1 for the South in Equation 3.5, we get

$$E(Y_{it}) = (\beta_0^N + \delta_0) + (\beta_1^N + \delta_1) Year_{it} \qquad (3.7)$$

because $\beta_0^N = \beta_0^*$ and $\beta_1^N = \beta_1^*$. Hence, the South's intercept (β_0^S) and slope (β_1^S) are $\beta_0^N + \delta_0$ and $\beta_1^N + \delta_1$, respectively. Thus:

$$\delta_0 = \beta_0^S - \beta_0^N \qquad (3.8)$$

and

$$\delta_1 = \beta_1^S - \beta_1^N. \qquad (3.9)$$

If both δs are nonzero and positive, opposition to interracial marriage is greater in the South initially $(\delta_0 > 0 \rightarrow \beta_0^S > \beta_0^N)$, and $\beta_1^S > \beta_1^N$, so the regional difference is increasing. If both δs are negative, opposition is greater in the Nonsouth initially $(\delta_0 < 0)$, and $\beta_1^N > \beta_1^S$, so the regional difference is increasing. In short, the trends diverge when the δs have the same sign. Convergence occurs when the δs have opposing signs.

The same principles hold for "effect coding," that is, coding S in Equation 3.5 as 1 for the South and -1 for the Nonsouth. (Under dummy coding, β_1^* is the trend for the reference group; under effect coding, β_1^* is the average of the trends for the South and Nonsouth.) Substituting $+1$ and -1 for South and Nonsouth respectively in Equation 3.5 yields $\beta_0^S = \beta_0 + \delta_0$, $\beta_1^S = \beta_1 + \delta_1$, $\beta_0^N = \beta_0 - \delta_0$, and $\beta_1^N = \beta_1 - \delta_1$. Thus:

$$\delta_0 = (\beta_0^S - \beta_0^N)/2 \qquad (3.10)$$

and

$$\delta_1 = (\beta_1^S - \beta_1^N)/2 \quad \text{[under effect coding]}. \qquad (3.11)$$

A Warning About Self-Selection

In some instances, groups diverge because recruitment into the groups is related to the variable of interest. For example, suppose we classify Protestants as "conservative" and "liberal" based on their church affiliation, and we find that the two groups are becoming more polarized over the issue of prayer in public schools. In the absence of panel data, it is hard to know how to interpret this polarization. Are conservative Protestants in fact becoming more pro-prayer relative to liberal Protestants? Or is the causal direction reversed, with attitudes toward prayer influencing one's church affiliation? In other words, as prayer in public schools has become a more salient public issue, perhaps it has become an increasingly important criterion for selecting a church—and that could account for the observed polarization, as members of liberal churches who favor prayer in public schools switch to conservative churches and members of conservative churches who oppose prayer in public schools switch to liberal churches.

A variant of this problem is seen in the finding of a narrowing gap, South versus Nonsouth, in antiblack prejudice (Firebaugh & Davis, 1988). The reduction in regional differences could be "spurious" in the sense that it is due to migration, because migration has increased the proportion of southern residents with nonsouthern origins. To rule out that possibility, Firebaugh and Davis (1988) examined regional trends with and without migrants (and got similar results).

The important point is to be wary of the self-selection and migration problems when using repeated survey data to test for convergence or divergence of trends. The problem arises for groups that individuals can join or leave—religious groups, political parties, areal regions, and so on (but not ascribed groups such as age or gender)—because entry into and exit from those groups might be related to the dependent variable.

Empirical Example of the Divergence Model:
Testing the Age Polarization Thesis

There is concern today of an increasing rift between retirees and workers in the United States. Writers speculate that shifts in relative well-being of the two groups, combined with rising costs of entitlements to the elderly, have created a latent antagonism between the young and the old over Social Security, health care, education, and other areas in which interests are presumed to diverge. For example, Richard Reeves, a syndicated columnist, warned of a "confrontation coming in the United States between the demands of old people and the needs of the whole society" (quoted in Rosenbaum & Button, 1992, p. 385). In *Born to Pay*, Longman (1987, p. 2) claimed that "baby boomers are paying an unprecedented proportion of their incomes to support the current older generation in retirement" and warned that the "likely result, unless many fundamental trends are soon reversed, will be a war between the young and the old." (Gerontologists, by contrast, generally conclude that "Older people are nearly indistinguishable from younger adults on most issues" [Day, 1990, p. 47].)

Although a generational war is farfetched, it is possible that age-related divisions are deepening in the United States. The single-equation interaction model (Equation 3.5) applies here. If divisions are deepening, we expect same-signed δs—trend divergence.

I chose two dependent variables for testing the age polarization thesis: support for spending on education and support for spending on Social Security. These were chosen from a battery of items in the General Social Survey (GSS) introduced as follows:

> We are faced with many problems in this country, none of which can be solved easily or inexpensively. I'm going to name some of these problems, and for each one I'd like you to tell me whether you think we're spending too much money on it, too little money on it, or about the right amount of money. Are we spending too much, too little, or about the right amount on . . . improving the nation's education system? Social Security?

Support for education was first asked in 1973, whereas support for Social Security was first asked in 1984. I chose education because, in a cross-sectional study (the 1988 National Election Study), Vinovskis (1993, p. 62) found "quite strong" age differences, with the elderly expressing the lowest level of support for spending on education. I chose Social Security because of its centrality in the literature on generational equity (e.g., Donza, Duncan, Corcoran, & Groskind, 1988; Kotlikoff, 1992). For both dependent variables, I dichotomized the responses two ways—too much versus about right or too little, and too little versus about right or too much—and used logistic regression.

Tables 3.1 and 3.2 report the results. Retirees in fact are significantly less likely to support spending on education (δ_0 in Table 3.1): They are *more* likely to say that we spend too much and *less* likely to say that we spend too little. Contrary to the age polarization thesis, however, the difference (δ_1) has not become more pronounced over the past two decades. In every instance, the coefficients for initial difference and trend difference have opposing signs, indicating convergence, not divergence. In any case, the coefficients for trend difference (the δ_1) all fail to attain statistical significance, despite the relatively large sample. We conclude that the trends are parallel for retirees and workers. In sum, retirees *are* less supportive of spending on education, but there is no evidence of *deepening* division between the old and the young over the issue.

In the case of spending on Social Security (Table 3.2), conclusions depend on how the variable is dichotomized. Consistent with the generational conflict literature, retirees are less likely to say that we spend *too much* on Social Security; yet retirees are *also* less likely to say that we spend

TABLE 3.1

Trend Analysis of Support for Spending on Education, 1973-1993:
Logit Coefficients

| | Coding of Dependent Variable[a] | |
| | 1 = Spend | 1 = Spend |
Model	Too Much	Too Little
Model 1: Retirees vs. Others[b] ($N = 19,012$)		
Initial difference, retirees minus others[c] ($\hat{\delta}_0$ in Equation 3.5)	.978**	-.583**
Trend for retirees ($\hat{\beta}_1^* + \hat{\delta}_1$)	-.075**	.050**
Trend difference, retirees minus others[d] ($\hat{\delta}_1$)	-.019	.001
Model 2: Retirees vs. Paid Workers[b] ($N = 13,992$)		
Initial difference, retirees minus workers[c]	.947**	-.643**
Trend for retirees	-.075**	.050**
Trend difference, retirees minus workers[d]	-.013	.002

SOURCE: Data come from the General Social Surveys (Davis & Smith, 1994), excluding black oversamples.
a. "About right" is classified with "spend too little" in the first column of coefficients, and with "spend too much" in the second column of coefficients. First column: 1 = spend too much, 0 = about right or too little; second column: 1 = spend too little, 0 = about right or too much.
b. "Others" includes housekeepers and students, "paid workers" does not.
c. Difference in intercepts, where initial year (1973 here) is coded 0.
d. Difference in trends (slopes for year).
*$p < .05$; **$p < .001$.

TABLE 3.2

Trend Analysis of Support for Spending on Social Security, 1984-1993:
Logit Coefficients

| | Coding of Dependent Variable[a] | |
| | 1 = Spend | 1 = Spend |
Model	Too Much	Too Little
Model 1: Retirees vs. Others[b] ($N = 12,262$)		
Initial difference, retirees minus others[c]	-.879**	-.481**
Trend for retirees	.042	-.008
Trend difference, retirees minus others[d]	.078	.022
Model 2: Retirees vs. Paid Workers[b] ($N = 9,666$)		
Initial difference, retirees minus workers[c]	-1.029**	-.489**
Trend for retirees	.042	-.008
Trend difference, retirees minus workers[d]	.080	.029

SOURCE: Data are from General Social Surveys, excluding black oversamples.
a. "About right" is classified with "spend too little" in the first column of coefficients, and with "spend too much" in the second column of coefficients. First column: 1 = spend too much, 0 = about right or too little; second column: 1 = spend too little, 0 = about right or too much.
b. "Others" includes housekeepers and students, "paid workers" does not.
c. Difference in intercepts, where initial year (1984 here) is coded 0.
d. Difference in trends (slopes for year).
*$p < .05$; **$p < .001$.

too little on Social Security. Retirees, then, are significantly more likely to say that spending on Social Security is "about right," whereas others are more likely to choose either "too much" or "too little." The question of whether workers or retirees are more supportive of spending on Social Security depends on which tail of the distribution is examined.

Again, there is no evidence of divergence, at least not for the decade for which data are available (1984-1993). The interaction term δ_1 falls well short of statistical significance. Differences between retirees and workers, such as they are, have remained stable over the past decade.

Aside from testing the age polarization thesis, there are other obvious applications of the trend convergence/divergence model to contemporary social issues. For example, these days we hear about "gender gaps" in voting Republican, in environmental attitudes, in attitudes toward affirmative action, and so on. Are there such attitudinal and behavioral differences between the sexes, and, if so, have they increased in recent decades?

Fox and Firebaugh (1992) used the trend convergence/divergence model and the GSS to answer those questions with regard to sex differences in confidence in science. They found trend divergence: Women tend to express less confidence in science than men do, and the difference has increased over recent decades. In terms of the equations above, the coefficients for initial difference, δ_0, and trend difference, δ_1, have the same sign and are both statistically significant in their study; hence, their study points to the possibility of gender polarization, at least with regard to Americans' confidence in science.

4. DECOMPOSING AGGREGATE TRENDS

If we observe change in the relative proportions of Democrats and Republicans in the electorate, then we can infer that either individuals have switched parties or the population of the electorate has changed (presumably because older cohorts have died off and have been replaced by younger cohorts), or both. Put another way, the proximate sources of aggregate change are net change among individuals and population turnover. As a first step in the study of societal change, it is often useful to distinguish the contributions of individual change from those of change in membership. In this chapter, I describe and illustrate two methods for "proximate decomposition," that is, for decomposing a trend into those proximate sources. I conclude the chapter by describing the conditions under which societal change outpaces change for the average adult in the society.

Intracohort Change Versus Overall Change

Repeated surveys permit the study of social change. For example, white respondents who say they favor laws against black-white marriage declined from 35% in the 1974 GSS to 16% in the 1994 GSS. To determine the proximate cause of the change, it is useful to track this percentage *within* birth cohorts. If change within birth cohorts keeps pace with overall change, we can infer that the overall change derives from net individual change. On the other hand, if the percentage opposing interracial marriage does not change over time within birth cohorts, we can infer that the overall change derives from population turnover rather than from net individual change. Most often, overall change derives from both, and the trick is to determine the relative contribution of each.

Table 4.1 illustrates a useful way to array the data for comparing within-cohort change with overall change. The rows are birth cohorts, so by reading from left to right within rows we can observe intracohort shifts in whites' support for laws against interracial marriage. The intracohort shifts can be compared with shifts in the overall percentages: −7.3% for 1974 to 1984 and −11.5% for 1984 to 1994 (Table 4.1).

The overall percentages in Table 4.1 are a weighted average of the cohort percentages. In 1974, for example, 34.6% of respondents said that they favored laws against interracial marriage. This percentage is a weighted average of the cohort percentages in the first column: $[15.0 \times (307/1,243)]$ + $[24.3 \times (235/1,243)]$ + $[32.8 \times (201/1,243)]$ + $[45.2 \times (217/1,243)]$ + $[50.3 \times (159/1,243)]$ + $[71.4 \times (98/1,243)]$ + $[61.5 \times (26/1,243)] = 34.6$ (within rounding error). *Because overall percentage is a weighted average of the cohort percentages, change in overall percentage comes about because the cohort percentages change or the relative sizes (weights) of the cohorts change—or both.* In short, social change can be viewed as a function of intracohort change and change in the relative sizes of cohorts.

It is important to underscore why the setup in Table 4.1 is of particular interest. The issue arises because change in a column mean (including percentages, because percentages are means for dichotomous variables whose values are 0 and 100) can always be expressed as a weighted average of change in within-row means. Because that is always the case, what is so special about the setup in Table 4.1? The setup in Table 4.1 is strategic

TABLE 4.1

Within-Cohort and Total Change in Percentage of U.S. Adults[a]
Opposing Interracial Marriage: Ten-Year Intervals, 1974-1994

	1974		1984		1994		Change	
							1974-	1984-
Cohort	Percentage	N	Percentage	N	Percentage	N	1984	1994
1965-1974	—	—	—	—	8.5	258	—	—
1955-1964	—	—	14.9	302	8.9	404	—	−6.0*
1945-1954	15.0	307	13.9	267	10.1	346	−1.1	−3.8
1935-1944	24.3	235	27.4	179	16.5	218	+3.1	−10.9*
1925-1934	32.8	201	38.1	139	29.6	159	+5.3	−8.5
1915-1924	45.2	217	42.7	157	37.1	140	−2.5	−5.6
1905-1914	50.3	159	57.0	93	41.7	60	+6.7	−15.3
1895-1904	71.4	98	52.8	36	—	—	−18.6	—
1885-1894	61.5	26	—	—	—	—	—	—
All Cohorts	34.6	1,243	27.3	1,173	15.8	1,585	−7.3*	−11.5*
Average within-cohort change (weighted by size)							+0.4	−7.1*

a. Whites, age 20 and older.
*$p < .05$.

because, by choosing cohort as the row variable, it distinguishes individual-based social change from turnover-based change. Because individuals are embedded in cohorts, change within rows bears on individual change. To be sure, we do not know whether the change within rows comes from age effects or period effects (Equation 2.3, above; Firebaugh, 1990; Rodgers, 1990), but that is not the question here. The question is: How much social change comes from alteration of opinions, and how much comes from the replacement of older adults with younger ones? James Davis (1992, p. 274) puts it this way:

> There is no question that within a row we are talking about the same [group of] people . . . and within each column we are talking about distinct populations. It follows that the setup does distinguish change by "conversion" (persons in a given row altering their opinions) from change by replacement (altered composition in terms of the column variable).

The strategic value of the cohort-by-period data array is also recognized by Norpoth (1987), who uses that data array to address the party realignment question posed at the outset of this chapter. In his Table 4, Norpoth

(p. 386) employs the cohort-by-period array to argue that party realignment toward the Republican Party is "under way and here to stay" because of cohort replacement. In his words, "the historically unique surge toward the GOP among the young since 1980 . . . signals the prospect of a party realignment through generational replacement" (p. 376).

Norpoth (1987), however, stops short of actually decomposing the change in percentage Republican into its cohort replacement and conversion components. Norpoth's study is not unusual in that regard. Although social scientists often talk about cohort or "generational" replacement effects, they rarely estimate their magnitude. One reason might be that methods for estimating cohort replacement effects are not well known.

In the remainder of this chapter, I describe two methods—one based on regression, the other on algebra—for decomposing social change into its cohort replacement and within-cohort change components. Change in attitudes toward interracial marriage provides a convenient point of departure. By arraying the data as in Table 4.1, we see immediately that opposition to interracial marriage declined from 1974 to 1984 only because of population turnover; for 1984-1994, by contrast, much of the change is due to attitude change (more on this later). Average within-cohort change is near zero for 1974-1984. Change in the means is positive for some cohort categories and negative for others, but the difference is never statistically significant, so the overall decline of 7.3 percentage points is due to turnover in the population, as older, more prejudiced cohorts died off and were replaced by younger, less prejudiced ones.

Firebaugh and Davis (1988) arrived at the same conclusion for the 1972-1984 change in attitudes regarding interracial marriage. Instead of arraying the data as in Table 4.1, however, they used regression to decompose the overall trend. The next section describes the method they used.

Linear Decomposition

In this section, I describe what I have called "linear decomposition" (Firebaugh, 1989). Linear decomposition assumes linear and additive within-cohort change. In the next section, I describe an algebraic decomposition method that can be used when the linear-additive assumption is inappropriate. Linear decomposition is much easier, and in my experience the two methods have yielded similar conclusions when change is monotonic.

Linear and algebraic decomposition are methods for partitioning aggregate social change into the part resulting from cohort replacement and the part resulting from individual change. Although linear decomposition employs a cohort-by-period design, it does not begin by grouping adjacent birth years, as in Table 4.1, because linear decomposition treats cohort as continuous (year of birth). The point of departure for linear decomposition is not a standard cohort table, but rather a linear and additive regression model.

Because cohort tables (e.g., Table 4.1) are conventional in cohort analysis, it is important to note why I use a different point of departure for decomposing change. In the standard cohort table, row and column categories are the same width (e.g., both are 10 years wide) so that age or cohort groups can be followed diagonally in the table (in the cohort-by-period design, age groups move across the table diagonally). Thus, information is wasted because birth years are grouped to correspond to the column spacing. Diagonalizing age is not necessary, however, for decomposing change. In decomposition, the objective is to distinguish change resulting from individual conversion from change resulting from altered cohort composition. To accomplish that task, we need only to array the data so that we can follow cohorts over time. To follow cohorts over time, a simple data array—in which birth year is the row variable and period (time of measurement) is the column variable—will do. Hence, with respect to decomposing social change, it is not necessary to collapse the birth years into a few categories labeled "Depression cohort," "World War II cohort," and so on. If researchers decide to group, the grouping can be dictated by theory, without the stricture that the cohort groups match the time intervals between columns in a table.

How to Do Linear Decomposition

Linear decomposition consists of two steps. The first step uses regression to estimate annual change in Y within cohorts. Because we assume that the within-cohort slopes are linear and parallel (additive), we can estimate annual within-cohort change with the following regression equation:

$$Y_{it} = b_0 + b_1 Year_{it} + b_2 Cohort_{it} + e_{it} \qquad (4.1)$$

where Y_{it} is the value for Y for the ith respondent in the tth survey, b_0 is the estimated intercept, b_1 is the estimated within-cohort slope, b_2 is the estimated cross-cohort slope, $Year_{it}$ is year of measurement of the ith respondent in the tth survey, and $Cohort_{it}$ is birth year for the ith respondent in the tth survey. Note that the *cumulated* data set is used to estimate Equation 4.1. Because *Cohort* is in the equation, b_1 estimates change with cohort controlled for (*intra*cohort slope). The coefficient for *Cohort*, b_2, is the *inter*cohort, or cross-cohort, slope—the average difference between adjacent cohorts.[5] Linear decomposition assumes linearity for the cross-cohort and intracohort slopes.

The second step in linear decomposition uses the slopes in Equation 4.1 to estimate the contributions of intracohort change and cohort replacement to overall social change. Because b_1 estimates intracohort change per time unit (here, year), to estimate the total contribution of intracohort change to social change we multiply b_1 by number of years (or quarters, or months, depending on the time unit) from first survey to last survey:

$$\text{estimated contribution of intracohort change} = b_1(YR_T - YR_1) \quad (4.2)$$

where YR_T is the year of the final survey and YR_1 is the year of the first survey. Similarly, to estimate cohort replacement's contribution, we multiply b_2 by change in the birth-year mean from survey 1 to survey T:

$$\text{estimated contribution of cohort replacement} = b_2(C_T - C_1) \quad (4.3)$$

where C_T is average year of birth for the sample in the last survey and C_1 is average year of birth for the sample in the first survey. The two components typically do not sum exactly to aggregate change, but the discrepancy should not be large, because large discrepancies call into question the linear-additive assumption and signal that another decomposition method should be used.

Proof. This section demonstrates that the components given by Equations 4.2 and 4.3 in fact sum to total social change when relations are linear and additive. Consider the population model for the regression of Y on *Year* and *Cohort*:

$$Y_{it} = \beta_0 + \beta_1 Year_{it} + \beta_2 Cohort_{it} + \varepsilon_{it} \quad (4.4)$$

where the Greek letters denote population parameters. Again, β_1 is the annual within-cohort change in Y and β_2 is the cross-cohort slope. The cross-cohort slope reflects cohort differences in Y at a given point in time; if all cohorts have the same mean at any given point in time, β_2 is zero.

The mean of Y (denoted $\overline{Y}$) is the expected value of Y. Under the conventional assumption that $E(\varepsilon)=0$, it follows from Equation 4.4 that the Y-mean for the last survey (survey T) is

$$\overline{Y}_T = E(Y_{iT})$$

$$= E(\beta_0 + \beta_1 Year_{iT} + \beta_2 Cohort_{iT} + \varepsilon_{iT})$$

$$= \beta_0 + \beta_1 E(Year_{iT}) + \beta_2 E(Cohort_{iT}) + E(\varepsilon_{iT})$$

$$= \beta_0 + \beta_1 YR_T + \beta_2 C_T \tag{4.5}$$

where (to repeat) C_T is *average birth year* for respondents in the last survey. By the same logic, the Y-mean for the first survey is

$$\overline{Y}_1 = \beta_0 + \beta_1 YR_1 + \beta_2 C_1. \tag{4.6}$$

Aggregate change from the first survey to the last survey is the difference between (4.5) and (4.6):

$$\overline{Y}_T - \overline{Y}_1 = \beta_1(YR_T - YR_1) + \beta_2(C_T - C_1). \tag{4.7}$$

In the linear-additive case, then, a simple regression method can be used to partition total change, $\overline{Y}_T - \overline{Y}_1$, into its individual change and replacement components.

Empirical Example: Trend in Antiblack Prejudice

Firebaugh and Davis (1988) used linear decomposition in their study of trends in whites' prejudice toward blacks. First, they created a prejudice scale based on four items that were asked in the 1972, 1976, 1980, and 1984 General Social Surveys. The prejudice scale declined by 1.22 units from 1972 to 1984. Regressing the prejudice scale on *Year* and *Cohort* yields $b_1 = -0.0457$ and $b_2 = -0.0508$ (Firebaugh & Davis, 1988, Table 1). Substituting into Equation 4.2, the estimated contribution of intracohort change to the overall decline is $-0.0457 \times (1984 - 1972) = -0.55$.

Average birth year is 1927.2 for whites in the 1972 sample and 1939.8 for whites in the 1984 sample. Thus, from Equation 4.3, cohort replacement's contribution to overall change is estimated to be $-0.0508 \times (1939.8 - 1927.2) = -0.64$. Summing the two components yields -1.19, which is close to the observed change of -1.22. Our overall conclusion is that traditional antiblack prejudice declined in the United States from 1972 to 1984 and that half or more of the decline was due to the replacement of older, more prejudiced cohorts with younger, less prejudiced ones.

Algebraic Decomposition

In 1955, Evelyn Kitagawa demonstrated that the difference in rates (e.g., fertility rates) between two populations is a function of differences in (a) age-specific rates (see Das Gupta, 1993, for further decomposition of age-specific rates, and Smith, Morgan, & Koropeckyj-Cox, 1996, for an example), (b) differences in age composition, and (c) a product of the differences in (a) and (b). Here, instead of decomposing differences between different populations or nations at the same point in time, we want to decompose differences in the same nation at different points in time, and it is cohort composition, not age composition, that is our focus. Nevertheless, the logic is similar and, with some modification, Kitagawa's (1955) decomposition equations apply to the sort of partitioning we want to perform here.

First, we formalize the principle that a group mean is the sum of subgroup means weighted by their population share:

$$\mu = \Sigma_j p_j \mu_j \qquad (4.8)$$

where Σ is summation, μ_j is the mean on Y for the jth subgroup, and p_j is j's population share. (The p_j sum to 1.0.) It follows that the *difference* in the means ($\Delta\mu$) for groups 1 and 2 is

$$\Delta\mu = \mu_2 - \mu_1$$

$$= \Sigma_j p_{j2}\mu_{j2} - \Sigma_j p_{j1}\mu_{j1} \qquad (4.9)$$

where subscripts are added to distinguish groups 1 and 2. Algebraic manipulation of Equation 4.9 yields (Kitagawa, 1955):

$$\Delta\mu = \Sigma_j p_{j1}\Delta\mu_j + \Sigma_j \mu_{j1}\Delta p_j + \Sigma_j \Delta\mu_j \Delta p_j \qquad (4.10)$$

where $\Delta\mu_j$ is $\mu_{j2} - \mu_{j1}$, the difference between the two groups (e.g., nations) on the Y-mean for subgroup j, and Δp_j is $p_{j2} - p_{j1}$, the difference between the groups on the population shares for subgroup j. The three sums in Equation 4.10 represent the "rates" component, the composition component, and the product term, respectively.

Equation 4.10 is the fundamental decomposition equation for rates. To apply the rates decomposition equation to social change, we modify it as follows:

Let Δ denote *change over time*.
Let the subscripts 1 and 2 index surveys 1 and 2 instead of groups 1 and 2.
Let subscript j index the jth birth cohort.

The last modification is key. By letting j index birth cohort, the first term in Equation 4.10 becomes a weighted sum of $\Delta\mu_j$, change on Y within cohorts. This sum reflects the contribution of net individual change to overall change, because individual change is change within cohorts. If the population shares remain constant, Δp_j is zero for all cohorts, and the second and third terms drop out in Equation 4.10. In that case, all social change results from individual change, and the first sum in Equation 4.10 captures all the change, as it should.

The second term in Equation 4.10—a weighted sum of Δp_j, change in the cohorts' population shares—bears on cohort replacement. When individuals do not change, $\Delta\mu_j$ is zero, and the first and third terms drop out. In that case, all change is due to cohort replacement, and the second term captures all the change, as it should.

The third term in Equation 4.10 represents the part of $\Delta\mu$ that is not uniquely the result of either individual change or cohort replacement. This joint effect often is relatively small, because it is the product of two change terms. Das Gupta (1978) recommends that it be equally distributed among the first and second terms. This strategy yields a two-component equation:

$$\Delta\mu = \Sigma_j[(p_{j1} + p_{j2})/2]\Delta\mu_j + \Sigma_j[(\mu_{j1} + \mu_{j2})/2]\Delta p_j. \qquad (4.11)$$

Three-component (Equation 4.10) and two-component (Equation 4.11) decomposition differ only in the weights used for $\Delta\mu_j$ and Δp_j. Within-cohort change for the jth cohort is weighted by the cohort's *initial* population share—its population share at the first survey—in the three-component case and by the cohort's *average* population share $(p_{j1} + p_{j2})/2$ in the two-component case. Likewise, change in the population share for the jth cohort is weighted by the cohort's *initial* mean in the three-component case and by the cohort's *average* mean in the two-component case. (A variation on the two-component method will be given in a subsequent decomposition of change in gender role attitudes.)

It is important to stress that in the case of repeated surveys without a panel component, we can only follow birth cohorts—not individuals—over time. If mortality is related to Y within cohorts, then observed within-cohort change is a mixture of individual change and change resulting from mortality. In using within-cohort change to estimate individual change, then, we must assume that Y is unrelated to mortality within cohorts. The assumption is sometimes problematic, especially when decomposing trends for groups that might have different age-specific mortality rates. In decomposing the trend in the percentage of a population that is Republican, for example, we must assume that Republicans and non-Republicans have the same age-specific mortality rates. A reliable panel component in repeated surveys would enable researchers to check such assumptions. That is one of the reasons for including a panel component in repeated surveys.

Empirical Example:
Trend in Antiblack Prejudice Revisited

The 1972-1984 overall change in the antiblack prejudice scale is decomposed again, this time using algebra (see Firebaugh, 1992, for an SPSS program). The two-component method is used so that we can compare the results with those for linear decomposition. The estimates are as follows: individual change = –0.51 and cohort replacement = –0.71. The corresponding linear estimates are –0.55 and –0.64. Both methods therefore yield this essential conclusion: The decline in antiblack prejudice is due both to individual attitude change and to cohort replacement. The algebraic method attributes somewhat more of the change to cohort replacement, however.[6]

When Does Aggregate Change
Outpace Individual Change?

We are now in a position to better understand why adults often complain that change occurs too rapidly. When cohort replacement reinforces individual change, aggregate change outpaces average individual change, so from the perspective of the typical adult, social change in fact is "too fast."

The Same-Sign Slope Rule

Under the standard assumption of linear-additive effects, aggregate change outpaces individual change when the within- and cross-cohort slopes have the same sign. Consider Equation 4.7 again, noting that $YR_T - YR_1$ is always greater than zero and $C_T - C_1$ is greater than zero except in the improbable case in which mortality rates are higher for younger adults than they are for older adults. It follows immediately that individual change and cohort replacement contribute to change in the same direction when and only when β_1 and β_2 have the same sign. Thus, the *same-sign slope rule*: Assuming that mortality rates are higher for older adults than for younger ones, social change outpaces change for the average adult when the within- and cross-cohort slopes have the same sign.

Because β_1 and β_2 are functions of age effects, period effects, and cohort effects, the same-sign rule can be related to concepts that are familiar to most social scientists. Consider β_2, the cross-cohort slope. Why might adult cohorts differ? One popular argument is that adults born in different eras have different beliefs, attitudes, values, and so on because of the different historical conditions to which they have been exposed during their life span. Moreover, if attitudes are more pliable among the young and tend to harden with age (see Glenn, 1980), then cohort differences can arise because the *same* historical events have *greater impact* on the young.

These ideas are prominent in two classic essays: Karl Mannheim's (1927/1952) "The Problem of Generations" and Norman Ryder's (1965) "The Cohort as a Concept in the Study of Social Change." Both assume that young people entering into adult society are more amenable to change than those already there, because people of more advanced age persist in the views they acquired when young. Mannheim (p. 298) wrote that "early impressions tend to coalesce into a natural view of the world," so "every concrete experience acquires its particular face and form from its relation to this primary stratum of experiences"—experiences that Mannheim thought took place at about age 17. Ryder (p. 844) wrote that "each new cohort makes fresh contact with the contemporary social heritage and carries the imprint of the encounter through life." In short, "cohorts develop distinctive meaning-giving universes early in life and seem to maintain them throughout adulthood" (Lesthaege & Surkyn, 1988, p. 40).

The "distinctive meaning-giving universes" of cohorts produce social change as older cohorts are replaced by later ones. This is what Comte (1839/1974, Book 6, chap. 6, p. 518) meant when he wrote that "our social progression rests upon death." Ryder (1965) argued further that social change, once begun, is likely to continue because of a sort of built-in momentum. The momentum derives from the twin processes of "demographic metabolism" (p. 843)—the continuous winnowing of old birth cohorts and adding of new ones—and cohort differences. Change portends change if "a cohort meaning is implanted" (p. 861). To implant cohort meaning, "transformations of the social world must modify people of different ages in different ways" and "the effects of these transformations [must be] persistent" (p. 861). Because social transformations have greater impact on the young, change is spread over the future as older, less affected cohorts gradually die off and younger, more affected cohorts are added to adult society.

In short, social transformation has both an immediately observed effect (because it presumably affects at least some members of the extant population) and a delayed effect. In a hypothetical world of no cohort succession, the effects of social transformation would be immediate or, if delayed, delayed only because it takes time for an effect to diffuse through the population. In the real world, cohort succession "magnifies" the impact of social transformations not by diffusion but by changing the composition of the population from less affected to more affected cohorts.

In Ryder's model, then, aggregate change outpaces average individual change because cohort effects complement period effects. From the same-sign rule, we can derive more formally the general age-period-cohort conditions under which aggregate change outpaces individual change.

The Same-Sign Slope Rule and Age-Period-Cohort Effects

The signs of the within- and cross-cohort slopes depend on the signs and relative magnitudes of age, period, and cohort effects. This is best seen by again considering the linear-additive model with all three effects:

$$Y_{it} = \beta_0 + \beta_P Period_{it} + \beta_C Cohort_{it} + \beta_A Age_{it} + \varepsilon_{it}. \qquad (4.12)$$

Although the model depicted by Equation 4.12 cannot be estimated, it can be used to determine what the same-sign rule means in terms of age-period-cohort effects. Substituting *Period − Cohort* for *Age* in Equation 4.12 gives

$$Y_{it} = \beta_0 + (\beta_P + \beta_A)Period_{it} + (\beta_C - \beta_A)Cohort_{it} + \varepsilon_{it}. \qquad (4.13)$$

By comparing Equation 4.13 with Equation 4.4, we get this key result:

$$\text{Within-cohort slope: } \beta_1 = \beta_P + \beta_A \qquad (4.14)$$

$$\text{Cross-cohort slope: } \beta_2 = \beta_C - \beta_A. \qquad (4.15)$$

(When contemplating the signs of age and cohort effects, keep in mind that age and cohort are coded in opposite directions; at a given point in time, those coded lower on age will be coded higher on cohort, because they were born later.)

From Equations 4.14 and 4.15, it is a straightforward matter to determine when β_1 and β_2 will have the same sign in linear-additive models. The cross-cohort slope, β_2, is positive when $\beta_C > \beta_A$ and negative when $\beta_C < \beta_A$. Thus, in the case of positive individual change—$\beta_1 > 0$—aggregate change outpaces individual change when, and only when, $\beta_C > \beta_A$. This condition places no restrictions on the signs of the age and cohort effects; they could both be negative, yet the cross-cohort slope will be positive as long as β_A is to the left of β_C on the number line ($\beta_A < \beta_C$). In the case of negative individual change—$\beta_1 < 0$—aggregate change outpaces individual change when, and only when, $\beta_C < \beta_A$. Again, there are no restrictions on the signs of β_C and β_A; what matters is their *relative location* on the number line.

In sum, under the standard assumption of linearity and additivity, when aggregate and individual change are in the same direction, aggregate change outpaces individual change when and only when:

$\beta_C > \beta_A$ in the case of upward trends

and

$\beta_C < \beta_A$ in the case of downward trends.

Empirical Example of the Rule:
Gender Role Attitudes

The massive entry of women into the paid labor force in recent decades is the sort of social transformation that most likely has greater impact on the attitudes of the young. With respect to gender role attitudes in the United States, then, one expects cohort effects that complement period effects, in line with Ryder.

To verify these expectations, I use data for the four gender role items repeated most often in the General Social Survey (Table 4.2). The first item pertains to the issue of women in the paid labor force (WORK), the next two items pertain to women in politics (PRES, POLI), and the fourth item appears to contain both a politics and a "domesticity" dimension (HOME). "Weighted" in Table 4.2 refers to adjustments made for the GSS undercount of married people.[7] Weighting has no effect, however, so in subsequent tables I report only the unweighted results.

In 1972, 65% of respondents said they approved of a woman earning money if she had a husband capable of supporting her; in 1988, 80% approved (Table 4.2). A similar pattern emerges for the other items about women's roles. (It is interesting that these percentages do not differ by sex of respondent [not shown].) In 1972, 74% said they would vote for a

TABLE 4.2

Change in Gender Role Attitudes in the United States

	1972 Mean[a]	1988 Mean	Change
WORK: Do you approve or disapprove of a married woman earning money in business or industry if she has a husband capable of supporting her? (1 = approve, 0 = disapprove)			
Unweighted sample	.654	.804	.150*
Weighted sample	.652	.807	.155*
PRES: If your party nominated a woman for president, would you vote for her if she were qualified for the job? (1 = yes)			
Unweighted sample	.737	.879	.142*
Weighted sample	.737	.879	.142*
POLI: Tell me if you agree or disagree with this statement: Most men are better suited emotionally for politics than are most women (1 = disagree)			
Unweighted sample	.532	.667	.135*
Weighted sample	.530	.670	.140*
HOME: Do you agree or disagree with this statement: Women should take care of running their homes and leave running the country up to men (1 = disagree)			
Unweighted sample	.644	.788	.144*
Weighted sample	.643	.791	.148*

a. 1974 mean for POLI and HOME.
*$p < .0001$.

qualified female nominee for president; in 1988, 88% said they would. In 1974, slightly over half of respondents disagreed with the statement that "most men are better suited emotionally for politics than are most women"; in 1988, about two-thirds disagreed. Those disagreeing with the statement that "women should take care of running their homes and leave running the country up to men" increased from 64% in 1974 to 79% in 1988.

Is this an instance in which the rate of change overall is outpacing change in attitudes for the average adult? Table 4.3 reports estimates of the within- and cross-cohort slopes for the four gender role items. The items are dichotomies, so statistical considerations dictate the use of logistic regression. The within- and cross-cohort slopes have the same sign for all four items. (Ordinary least squares regression yields the same results.) Based

34

TABLE 4.3
Estimated Change in Gender Role Attitudes Within and Across Cohorts:
Logit Coefficients

Gender Role Measure	Within-Cohort ($\hat{\beta}_1$)	Cross-Cohort ($\hat{\beta}_2$)
WORK 1972-1988 ($N = 14,376$)	.029*	.032*
PRES 1972-1988 ($N = 14,188$)	.022*	.031*
POLI 1974-1988 ($N = 11,058$)	.029*	.024*
HOME 1974-1988 ($N = 12,665$)	.029*	.035*

*$p < .01$.

TABLE 4.4
Estimated Change in Gender Role Attitudes Among Surviving Adults,
1972[74]-1988

	Change	
Gender Role Item	Overall[a]	Among Survivors[b]
WORK	.150	.087
PRES	.142	.089
POLI	.135	.036
HOME	.144	.065

a. From Table 4.2.
b. Average change among surviving adults. See text for calculation method.

on the conditions just derived, then, gender role ideology is changing at a
faster pace for adult society as a whole than it is for the typical adult.

Algebraic decomposition leads to the same conclusion. For each of the four
items, the egalitarian response was given by about 15% more respondents in
1988 than in 1972 or 1974.[8] We can decompose algebraically to see how this
15 percentage-point change compares to the change for surviving adults.

Because we want change for survivors, we weight within-cohort change,
$\mu_{j2} - \mu_{j1}$, by cohort population share at time 2, not time 1. We use $\Sigma_j p_{j2}(\mu_{j2} - \mu_{j1})$ to estimate change for the average surviving adult.[9]

Table 4.4 reports the results. For all four items, average change for survivors
lags substantially behind overall change. (Because the mean for survivors is
further from the ceiling than is the mean for all adults, the slower change for

survivors cannot be attributed to ceiling effects.) Overall, those approving "of a married woman earning money in business or industry if she has a husband capable of supporting her" increases 15 percentage points, yet for surviving adults, the increase is 8.7 percentage points. In 1988, 88% said they would vote for a qualified woman for president if she were nominated by their party, an increase of 14 percentage points from 1972; for surviving adults, the increase is 8.9 percentage points. The other items exhibit a similar pattern.

In short, Table 4.4 verifies the prediction of the same-sign slope rule. Gender role attitudes in the United States are changing faster for adult society in general than they are for the typical adult.

Concluding Remark

The question of how micro- and macroprocesses link is a perennial topic of discussion in sociology (Alexander, Geisen, Munch, & Smelser, 1987; Coleman, 1986; Durkheim, 1895/1938). The same-sign slope rule for the linear-additive case bears on that link by providing insight into why aggregate change sometimes deviates from individual change. (In the real world, of course, effects might be nonlinear and interactive [Elder, 1974], yet the linear-additive ideal type is a useful place to begin.) The insight is that adult societies change faster than the average adult in them when the within- and cross-cohort slopes have the same sign. Stated in terms of age and cohort effects, the same-sign slope rule means that societal change outpaces average individual change when $\beta_C > \beta_A$ in the case of upward trends and when $\beta_C < \beta_A$ in the case of downward trends.

5. A GENERAL MODEL FOR DECOMPOSING AGGREGATE CHANGE

The previous chapter described two methods for separating out the cohort replacement component of social change. In isolating the cohort replacement component, we seek only to account for the *locus* of observed change: Does the change derive from population turnover or from individual change? Because the objective is to determine locus of change, that type of decomposition does not add variables in an attempt to explain why individuals change or why cohorts differ.

This chapter addresses the question of change in terms of causal variables. The objective is to present a general model for accounting for aggregate change in one variable from time 1 to time 2 in terms of change in the *levels* and *effects* of other variables over the same time period. The model assumes only two measurement points (not T points, as in linear decomposition). Because the model is equivalent in form to the well-known regression standardization model, there is less need to illustrate it with original analysis; I rely on existing studies. The studies I use are from the political science literature on the puzzling post-1960 decline in voter turnout in American elections.

The Model

Consider the simple linear regression model where Y is a function of X:

$$Y = \alpha + \beta X + \varepsilon. \tag{5.1}$$

As noted earlier (Equation 4.5), the mean of Y is its expected value:

$$\overline{Y} = E(Y)$$

$$= E(\alpha + \beta X + \varepsilon)$$

$$= \alpha + \beta \overline{X} \tag{5.2}$$

under the conventional assumption that $E(\varepsilon) = 0$. Equation 5.2 confirms that a regression line goes through the point $(\overline{X}, \overline{Y})$; hence, we can calculate the mean of Y from the mean of X by multiplying the mean of X by the slope and adding the intercept. More to the point here, Equation 5.2 tells us that we can express the mean of Y in terms of (a) the mean of X, (b) the slope of the X-Y relationship, and (c) the intercept.

Because $\overline{Y}$ can be expressed in terms of $\overline{X}$, regression slope, and intercept, it follows that change in $\overline{Y}$ can be expressed in terms of change in $\overline{X}$, change in slope, and change in intercept. Adding subscripts to index time, from Equation 5.2 it follows that change in the mean of Y is:

$$\overline{Y}_2 - \overline{Y}_1 = (\alpha_2 + \beta_2 \overline{X}_2) - (\alpha_1 + \beta_1 \overline{X}_1)$$

$$= (\alpha_2 - \alpha_1) + (\beta_2 \overline{X}_2 - \beta_1 \overline{X}_1)$$

$$= (\alpha_2 - \alpha_1) + (\beta_2 \overline{X}_2 - \beta_1 \overline{X}_1) + (\beta_2 \overline{X}_1 - \beta_2 \overline{X}_1)$$
$$+ (\beta_1 \overline{X}_2 - \beta_1 \overline{X}_2) + (\beta_1 \overline{X}_1 - \beta_1 \overline{X}_1)$$

$$= (\alpha_2 - \alpha_1) + (\beta_2 - \beta_1)\overline{X}_1 + \beta_1(\overline{X}_2 - \overline{X}_1) + (\beta_2 - \beta_1)(\overline{X}_2 - \overline{X}_1)$$

$$= \Delta\alpha + \Delta\beta\overline{X}_1 + \beta_1\Delta\overline{X} + \Delta\beta\Delta\overline{X}. \qquad (5.3)$$

In sum, change in $\overline{Y}$ can be partitioned into four components reflecting change in the intercept ($\Delta\alpha$), change in the *means* of the explanatory variables ($\Delta\overline{X}$), and change in the *effects* of the explanatory variables ($\Delta\beta$). (Other decompositions are possible by summing various combinations of the four components in Equation 5.3 to form three components or even two components.) Observe that, unlike the regression method described in Chapter 4, the decomposition here is exact: The components sum to change in $\overline{Y}$.

Readers familiar with regression standardization will recognize that Equation 5.3 is equivalent in form to the decomposition equation in regression standardization (e.g., Sobel, 1983, Equation 4). *The difference is that here the subscripts 1 and 2 denote time, as opposed to group.* Regression standardization, as the name suggests, uses regression to standardize distributions. Often, the objective is to standardize the distributions for two groups to purge them of compositional differences that account for some of the group differences in the dependent variable. For example, studies of sex discrimination in income often employ regression standardization to adjust for differences between female and male workers with regard to age, hours worked per week, labor force experience, and so on.

Because the model I propose for partitioning aggregate change over time (Equation 5.3) is formally equivalent to the regression standardization model for partitioning the difference between two group means, problems inherent in the regression standardization method also apply when Equation 5.3 is used to decompose change. That observation is important, because regression standardization is bedeviled by the "origin-dependence" or "location-shift" problem (Clogg & Eliason, 1986; Firebaugh, 1992; Jones & Kelley, 1984). The problem is this: By adding a constant to X, we change the size of the first two components in Equation 5.3. In fact, unless X has a defensible zero point, the contribution of changing intercepts ($\Delta\alpha$) to aggregate change can be made arbitrarily large or small simply by shifting the origin of X, that is, by adding a constant to X.

To better appreciate the scope of the problem, note first that the third and fourth components in Equation 5.3 are *not* origin-dependent. The third component, $\beta_1 \Delta \overline{X}$, is the part of the overall change in the Y-mean that is uniquely the result of change in the mean of the explanatory variable. The fourth component, $\Delta \beta \Delta \overline{X}$, is the part of the overall change resulting from the joint effect of changing slope and changing mean. These components are not origin-dependent because adding a constant to X does not affect the *difference* in the X-means, $\Delta \overline{X}$.

Adding a constant to X does change the mean of X, however, so unless $\Delta \beta = 0$, adding a constant affects the second component, $\Delta \beta \overline{X}_1$. It follows that adding a constant also affects $\Delta \alpha$, because the equation must balance: From Equation 5.3, $\Delta \alpha = \Delta \overline{Y} - (\Delta \beta \overline{X}_1 + \beta_1 \Delta \overline{X} + \Delta \beta \Delta \overline{X})$, and $\Delta \overline{Y}$, $\beta_1 \Delta \overline{X}$, and $\Delta \beta \Delta \overline{X}$ are unaffected by the addition of a constant to X (but $\Delta \beta \overline{X}_1$ *is* affected), so obviously $\Delta \alpha$ also is affected.

In short, unless the effect of X is constant ($\Delta \beta = 0$), $\Delta \alpha$—the part of the change in Y that is unexplained by change in the level and effect of X—can be gerrymandered by adding a constant to X. By adding the appropriate constant to X, for example, we could make $\Delta \alpha = 0$, and thus claim that change in $\overline{Y}$ is due entirely to change in the level and effect of X. Or we could add a constant to X that would make the difference in the intercepts equivalent to the difference in the $\overline{Y}$ (that is, we could make the other three components sum to zero). With the very same data and variables, therefore, one researcher could claim that change in the level and effect of X explains *all* of the change in the Y mean ($\Delta \alpha = 0$) while another researcher could claim that change in the level and effect of X on net explains *none* of the change in the Y mean ($\Delta \alpha = \Delta \overline{Y}$, so the contributions associated with X sum to zero).

There are two basic strategies for dealing with the problem. The best strategy is to choose Xs with non-arbitrary zero points, that is, to choose measures that are ratio scale. Zero is a fixed point in a ratio variable, so the intercept occurs at a fixed point, and an unambiguous decomposition is possible. When ratio measurement is not possible, researchers can combine the first two components in Equation 5.3, yielding the following components (Sobel, 1983):

$\Delta \alpha + \Delta \beta \overline{X}_1$, the contribution of changing parameters (note the different use of the term "changing parameters" here, to refer to change in the intercepts as well as change in the slopes)

$\beta_1 \Delta \overline{X}$, the contribution of changing level of X

$\Delta \beta \Delta \overline{X}$, the joint contribution of change in the level and effect of X.

The bottom line is that ratio measurement is required to disentangle the effect of changing intercepts from the effect of changing slopes. Lest that be viewed as a defect of the method, it should be noted that the phrase "effect of changing intercepts" has no meaningful *substantive* interpretation when the intercept can be moved around arbitrarily. When the location of the intercept is arbitrary (as in the case of interval-scale Xs), $\Delta\alpha$ is nothing more than a term that balances Equation 5.3.

Multivariate Decomposition

Generalizing the decomposition in Equation 5.3 to the case of multiple explanatory variables is straightforward. For ease of exposition, it is convenient to use vector notation. Let $\mathbf{X}$ denote a $1 \times q$ row vector of regressors and β denote a $q \times 1$ column vector of parameters. Then the mean of Y can be expressed as $\overline{Y} = E(\alpha + \mathbf{X}\beta + \varepsilon) = \alpha + \overline{\mathbf{X}}\beta$, where $\overline{\mathbf{X}}$ is a $1 \times q$ vector of X-means. Again adding subscripts to index time, it follows that *change* in the mean of Y from time 1 to time 2 is

$$\overline{Y}_2 - \overline{Y}_1 = (\alpha_2 + \overline{\mathbf{X}}_2\beta_2) - (\alpha_1 + \overline{\mathbf{X}}_1\beta_1)$$

$$= (\alpha_2 - \alpha_1) + \overline{\mathbf{X}}_1(\beta_2 - \beta_1) + (\overline{\mathbf{X}}_2 - \overline{\mathbf{X}}_1)\beta_1 + (\overline{\mathbf{X}}_2 - \overline{\mathbf{X}}_1)(\beta_2 - \beta_1)$$

$$= \Delta\alpha + \overline{\mathbf{X}}_1\Delta\beta + \Delta\overline{\mathbf{X}}\beta_1 + \Delta\overline{\mathbf{X}}\Delta\beta. \tag{5.4}$$

Decomposition using Equation 5.4 should not be confused with decomposition using the linear decomposition method described in Chapter 4. First, the Equation 5.4 model is based on two cross sections, whereas the Chapter 4 model employs all the cross sections. Second, the decomposition model in Equation 5.4 permits changes in the effects of the explanatory variables, whereas the Chapter 4 model assumes constant parameters (including intercepts) over time. If we assumed $\Delta\alpha = \Delta\beta = 0$ in Equation 5.4, then that model would reduce to the $\Delta\overline{Y} = \Delta\mathbf{X}\beta$ form of the Chapter 4 model (see Equation 4.7). Third, the decomposition in Equation 5.4 is a flexible model, with no fixed number of regressors. The decomposition in Chapter 4, by contrast, is designed for the specific purpose of separating the effect of cohort replacement from the effect of within-cohort change, so the same regressors—measurement year and birth year—are always used.

Example: Declining Voter Turnout in the United States

To illustrate a potential application of the decomposition framework provided by Equation 5.4, consider trends in voter turnout in national elections in the United States over the past several decades. Voting rates in the United States declined over the three decades following the 1960 Kennedy-Nixon presidential race, before rebounding in the 1992 election (Abramson et al., 1994). That long-term decline is particularly intriguing in light of the direction of change in many of the individual-level determinants of voter turnout. For example, the education level of the electorate has increased since 1960, and there is a strong positive relationship between formal education and likelihood of voting (Wolfinger & Rosenstone, 1980). Based on trends in education, then, one would have expected turnout to increase, not decline.

A prodigious empirical literature (see Abramson et al., 1994, chap. 4, for an overview) attempts to shed light on the American turnout "puzzle" (Brody, 1978), the puzzle of a declining turnout rate in the face of an increasingly better-educated and more affluent electorate and an easing of voter registration requirements. These studies of the turnout puzzle draw on a long and venerable tradition of empirical studies of electoral participation in America (e.g., Campbell, Converse, Miller, & Stokes, 1960; Kleppner, 1982; Merriam & Gosnell, 1924; Verba & Nie, 1972; Wolfinger & Rosenstone, 1980). Studies of participation have generated a long list of demographic and attitudinal correlates of voting behavior (Bennett & Bennett, 1987), and from this list Abramson and Aldrich (1982) identify two as bearing the most directly on turnout decline: "The decline in electoral participation results largely from two basic attitudinal trends: the weakening of party loyalties among the American electorate and declining beliefs about government responsiveness" (p. 502). The thorough analyses by Teixeira (1987, 1992) reach the same conclusions as well as adding the point that turnout decline is also tied to a "substantial decline in social connectedness, as manifested in a younger, less married, and less church-going electorate" (Teixeira, 1992, p. 57).

The agreement between the Abramson and Aldrich (1982) and Teixeira (1987, 1992) studies is notable because they use different decomposition methods. Both use the cumulated National Election Studies (beginning with 1960) and use dummy variables for election year to model change over time. The Abramson-Aldrich analysis, however, employs a changing-slopes model that allows the effects of their two explanatory variables to change over time. Teixeira uses many more explanatory variables but (aside from a few supplementary regressions) assumes that their effects are constant over time; that is, he assumes $\Delta\beta = 0$. By substituting $\Delta\beta = 0$ into Equation 5.4 above, we can better appreciate the implications of Teixeira's decompositions for the difference between voter turnout in any two elections:

$$\overline{Y}_2 - \overline{Y}_1 = \Delta\alpha + \overline{\mathbf{X}}_1\Delta\beta + \Delta\overline{\mathbf{X}}\beta_1 + \Delta\overline{\mathbf{X}}\Delta\beta$$

$$= \Delta\alpha + \Delta\overline{\mathbf{X}}\beta_1 \text{ for } \Delta\beta = 0. \tag{5.5}$$

In other words, Teixeira's method partitions voter decline into (a) $\Delta\overline{\mathbf{X}}\beta_1$, a compositional effect (the part due to changes in the means of the Xs), and (b) $\Delta\alpha$, change not accounted for by the Xs.

In decomposing decline in voter turnout, Teixeira (1987, 1992) examined the change in the intercepts $(\Delta\alpha)$ as Xs were added to the model (observe that $\Delta\alpha = (\overline{Y}_2 - \overline{Y}_1) - \Delta\overline{\mathbf{X}}\beta_1$ in his model). "If these coefficients were significantly decreased by the addition of a given variable, this would be a sign that distributional change on that variable had a substantial role in turnout decline" (Teixeira, 1987, p. 45, and 1992, p. 196). By comparing Equation 5.5 with Equation 5.4, we note that this interpretation assumes constant $\mathbf{X}$-effects $(\Delta\beta = 0)$. *If* the effects of $\mathbf{X}$ are constant over time, then it is valid to interpret the difference between the time 1 and time 2 intercepts as the difference in the Y-means that is not accounted for by the explanatory variables.[10]

As an alternative to Teixeira's additive decomposition model of turnout decline, we could use the model in Equation 5.4. The model in Equation 5.4 is more general because it includes the contribution (if any) of the changing effects of the explanatory variables. Consider the decline in voter turnout over the eight presidential elections from 1960 to 1988. We could decompose the decline in one step as follows:

$$\overline{Y}_{88} - \overline{Y}_{60} = \Delta\alpha + \overline{\mathbf{X}}_{60}\Delta\beta + \Delta\overline{\mathbf{X}}\beta_{60} + \Delta\overline{\mathbf{X}}\Delta\beta_{60}. \tag{5.6}$$

In other words, we decompose by using only the data for 1960 and 1988, and we ignore the data for the intervening six elections. (Again, if some Xs are not ratio scale, the first and second components in Equation 5.6 would be combined.) Alternatively, we could use the data for all eight elections by decomposing the change sequentially—first decompose the change from 1960 to 1964, then the change from 1964 to 1968, and so on—and sum. I recommend the second method, even though it is more laborious.

Conclusion

This chapter has presented a general model that partitions aggregate change in Y in terms of change in the *levels* of the explanatory variables (compositional effect), change in the *effects* of the explanatory variables, and change in the intercept. This model is intended to serve as a template for studying social change. Researchers must resist the temptation to apply the method mechanically, however. *A decomposition is only as informative as the explanatory variables on which it is based.* For example, we could "account for" the decline in voter turnout by applying the decomposition equation to any variables that are correlated with voting and have exhibited an upward or downward trend over the past three decades. Such mechanical applications of the method might well yield statistically significant results yet tell us nothing useful about the social world.

6. DETECTING CHANGE IN INDIVIDUAL-LEVEL RELATIONSHIPS

This book is about the analysis of social change. To this point, I have focused on aggregate change, but the term "social change" sometimes refers to changing *relationships* at the *individual level*. This chapter describes how simple regression models can be used with repeated survey data to determine whether or not the effects of explanatory variables are changing over time.

The Changing-Parameter Model

The term "changing-parameter model" in this chapter refers to a model designed to study $\Delta\beta$, the changing effects of the Xs. As described in the previous chapter, researchers can study changing parameters as one component of aggregate social change. In this chapter, however, I focus on the study of changing parameters per se, as opposed to the study of their contribution to larger social change. Because changing individual-level effects often are interesting in their own right, analyses using changing-parameter models can stand alone.

I use interaction terms to model changing X-effects. An interaction effect occurs when the effect of one variable on another depends on the level of some third variable Z. Here Z is time itself. To say that the effect of X

changes over time is to say that the effect of X depends on time—an example of interaction in the classic sense of the term.

The interaction terms I use have the form X times D_{YR}, where D_{YR} is a dummy variable coded 1 for a given year (or month, or week, depending on the frequency of measurement). As we will see, the explanatory variable, X, can be either continuous or categorical.

Suppose we want to know whether the determinants of political party identification in the United States are different in 1994 from what they were 20 years earlier. We could do two parallel analyses—one for 1974 data and one for 1994 data—and compare the coefficients. With that approach, it would not be immediately obvious which differences are statistically significant and which are not. To determine whether or not *differences* between sample coefficients in separate samples (here, separate years) are statistically significant, we must perform the appropriate significance tests. One strategy is to perform separate regression analyses for each of the samples and use the formulas given in Long and Miethe (1988, pp. 125-129) to calculate t tests for the differences of interest. With repeated survey data, however, that strategy is seldom necessary, because data collectors most often merge new samples with prior samples. With such cumulated data sets, it is generally much easier to test for changing parameters by estimating a single model with interaction terms, and that is the strategy I describe here.

General Form of the Model

Expressed in vector notation, the changing-parameter model is

$$E(Y) = \alpha + \gamma D_{YR} + \mathbf{X}\beta + (\mathbf{X}D_{YR})\delta. \tag{6.1}$$

D_{YR} is a dummy variable for year, $\mathbf{X}$ is a vector of predictor variables other than D_{YR}, and β and δ are vectors of parameters. If there are q variables in vector $\mathbf{X}$, then $\mathbf{X}$ and $\mathbf{X}D_{YR}$ each has dimension $1 \times q$, and β and δ each has dimension $q \times 1$.

Equation 6.1 states the model in its most general form, with interaction terms for each of the regressors. I present it only to show the range of the model. In applying the model, researchers most often will want to restrict the interaction terms to some *subset* of Xs, especially if the list of regressors is long. The principle for including an interaction term in a model is the same as the principle for including any regressor in a model: There must be some good reason (theory, prior evidence, or sensible argument) to believe that the variable has an effect. The greatest danger for abuse of the changing-parameter model lies with researchers on "fishing expeditions" for time-dependent effects. Interaction terms of this sort should be added only if there is reason to believe that a regressor's effect has changed over time. If interaction terms are added willy-nilly in a model with many regressors, some change in sample coefficients is likely to be statistically significant solely as the result of chance, and real change in parameters is likely to be missed as standard errors are inflated by multicollinearity.

It often helps to think in terms of a concrete issue. Consider the question of whether the determinants of political party identification changed between 1974 and 1994. The GSS includes this question: "Generally speaking, do you usually think of yourself as a Republican, Democrat, Independent, or what?" Codes range from 0 = *strong Democrat* to 6 = *strong Republican.* If we assume that this item taps a single dimension with Independent (coded 3) at the midpoint, we can use this variable as a measure of strength of Republican Party identification. To be consistent with subsequent illustrations, suppose we reverse the coding so 6 = *strong Democrat* and use the 1974 and 1994 GSS data to estimate this model:

$$E(Dem) = \alpha + \gamma D_{94} + \mathbf{X}\beta + (\mathbf{X}'D_{94})\delta \qquad (6.2)$$

where D_{94} is a dummy variable coded 1 for 1994, $\mathbf{X}$ is a $1 \times q$ vector of variables presumed to affect Democratic Party identification, and $\mathbf{X}'$ is a $1 \times p$ vector consisting of a subset of the variables in $\mathbf{X}$ (or, if p = q, then $\mathbf{X}' = \mathbf{X}$). The parameter α is the y-intercept for 1974, and $\alpha + \gamma$ is the intercept for 1994. The vector β consists of the parameters β_1, β_2, . . . , β_p, . . . , β_q for the q predictor variables $X_1, X_2, \ldots, X_p, \ldots, X_q$. The βs for $X_{p+1}, X_{p+2}, \ldots, X_q$ represent the direct effects of the predictor variables that are assumed to have the same effects in 1994 as they had in 1974. In contrast, the βs for $X_1, X_2, \ldots, X_p$ represent the direct effects of the predictor variables *in 1974* for those predictors whose effects are hypothesized to have changed from 1974 to 1994. Thus, β_1 is the direct effect of X_1 on Democratic identification in 1974, β_2 is the direct effect of X_2 in 1974, and so on, where the effects of $X_1, X_2, \ldots, X_p$ are hypothesized to be different in 1974 from what they were in 1994.

Observe that the changing-parameter model permits the effects of X to be time-dependent but includes no other types of interactions. In an application of Equation 6.2, for example, we might examine the effects of region (South vs. Nonsouth) and education on Democratic Party identification to determine whether the effects of region and education on party identification have changed in recent decades. In using Equation 6.2, we assume that the effect of education on party identification is the same in the South and the Nonsouth. That assumption can be tested, of course, by adding the interaction term Region × Education, where Region is a dummy variable. Because adding such interaction terms to a changing-parameter model is straightforward, I see no purpose in complicating the notation by adding such terms here. (Readers not familiar with such interaction terms can refer to a standard statistics text, such as Agresti and Finlay, 1986.) The point of the changing-parameter model is to determine whether X-effects have changed over time, so that is what we focus on here.

Significance Tests for Changing Effects

The interaction term $(\mathbf{X}'\mathbf{D}_{YR})\delta$ in Equation 6.2 is the key here, because it indicates whether or not the X-effects have changed over time. The vector $\mathbf{X}'\mathbf{D}_{94}$ consists of the variables $X_1 D_{94}, X_2 D_{94}, \ldots, X_p D_{94}$, where $X_1 D_{94}$ is X_1 for 1994 and zero for 1974, $X_2 D_{94}$ is X_2 for 1994 and zero for 1974, and so on. Thus, the vector δ represents 1974-1994 *change* in the effects of X_1, $X_2, \ldots X_p$ (for example, δ_1 is change in the effect of X_1). Because β_1 through β_p represent the direct effect of those Xs in 1974, it follows that X_1's direct effect *in 1994* is $\beta_1 + \delta_1$, X_2's direct effect in 1994 is $\beta_2 + \delta_2$, and so on.

We can test the statistical significance of the interaction terms individually and as a group, using the t test for individual coefficients and the F test for the interactions collectively (Long & Miethe, 1988). Package programs such as SPSS and SAS routinely provide the t-values for each of the coefficients. To test the interactions collectively, we estimate the X-effects again, this time without the interaction terms:

$$E(Dem) = \alpha_r + \gamma_r D_{94} + \mathbf{X}\beta_r \qquad (6.3)$$

where the subscript r is used to distinguish the parameters in the *reduced* model, represented by Equation 6.3, from those in the complete model, represented by Equation 6.2. The appropriate F test is

$$F = [(\text{SSE}_r - \text{SSE}_c)/p]/[\text{SSE}_c/(N - k)] \qquad (6.4)$$

where SSE_r is error sum of squares for the reduced model, SSE_c is error sum of squares for the complete model, k is number of parameters in the complete model, p is the number of interaction terms, and N is sample size. (Equation 6.4 can be reworked so that it is in terms of differences in R-squared, and some readers may be more familiar with that form. That is the form sometimes used in statistical packages such as SPSS.) Observe that if the interaction terms as a group fail to reduce the error sum of squares, then $SSE_c = SSE_r$, and $F = 0$, so F in this instance tests the null hypothesis that the interaction effects collectively are zero, that is, $\delta_1 = \delta_2 = \ldots = \delta_p = 0$ (Agresti & Finlay, 1986, p. 456). If we fail to reject this null hypothesis, then we conclude that the effects of the Xs are the same in 1974 and 1994. (In the case of logistic regression, significance tests are based on chi-square instead of F.)

Two Preliminary Examples

The interaction method for studying changing individual-level relationships is quite flexible. The Xs can be continuous or categorical or both. For continuous X, δ is the difference in *slopes*. For categorical X, δ is the difference in *category means* (or, when other explanatory variables are continuous, δ is the difference in intercepts).

In the case of categorical X, suppose we hypothesize that the regional difference (South vs. Nonsouth) in Democratic Party identification diminished between 1974 and 1994. We could test the hypothesis with the following model applied to combined 1974 and 1994 data:

$$E(Dem) = \alpha + \gamma D_{94} + \beta Region + \delta Region \times D_{94} \qquad (6.5)$$

where *Region* is a dummy variable coded 1 for those living in the South. Because D_{94} is coded 0 for 1974, β is the regional difference in 1974 and δ is the difference in the regional difference, 1994 minus 1974. Therefore, $\delta = 0$ means that the regional difference is the same in 1994 and 1974. For nonzero δ and β, the regional difference is larger in 1994 (than in 1974) when β and δ have the same sign, and it is smaller in 1994 when β and δ have opposing signs (except in the special case where δ is more than twice as large as β in absolute value). These principles hold whether *Region* is coded as 1 = South or as 1 = Nonsouth in Equation 6.5.

Now consider the case of continuous X. Suppose we hypothesize that the bivariate relationship between education and Democratic Party identification has changed in the United States. We could test that hypothesis with the following model:

$$E(Dem) = \alpha + \gamma D_{94} + \beta Educ + \delta Educ \times D_{94}. \tag{6.6}$$

The same principles hold in Equation 6.6 as in Equation 6.5. Education's effect is larger in 1994 than in 1974 when β and δ have the same sign; education's effect is the same when δ is zero (parallel slopes in 1974 and 1994); and education's effect is smaller in 1994 when β and δ have opposing signs, except where the magnitude of δ is more than twice that of β. The critical difference between Equations 6.6 and 6.5 is that the parameters in Equation 6.6 denote slopes and differences in slopes. In Equation 6.6, β is the slope for education in 1974 and δ is the difference in the education slopes, 1994 minus 1974.

Step-by-Step Illustration of Changing-Parameter Analysis: Race and Democratic Party Identification

It is well documented that African Americans are more likely than whites to identify with the Democratic Party and to vote for the Democratic candidate (Abramson et al., 1994, chap. 5). There is also some evidence that the race gap in Democratic Party identification is widening (Abramson et al., 1994, chap. 8). Here I employ changing-parameter models to compare GSS data for 1994 with GSS data 20 years earlier to test the hypothesis of a widening race gap in Democratic Party identification in the United States.

I begin with models with only a few variables. Simple is better here. The points I want to make are methodological, and I do not want readers to lose sight of those methodological points in a profusion of variables. Simple models suffice to illustrate the basic principles of changing-parameter models in repeated surveys. Once those principles are understood, it is an easy matter to add covariates to improve the model substantively, as I demonstrate. One should bear in mind that the primary point of the examples is to expound a method, not to advance a substantive area.

The Race Gap in Democratic Party Identification

Table 6.1 reports the percentages of white and black respondents, respectively, who identify themselves as "strong Democrats" in the 1973/1974 and 1994 General Social Surveys. The percentages are based on respondents with data on party identification, race, and four variables that are added later as covariates in a regression analysis: education, region, gender, and age ($N = 5,581$). Because the 1994 GSS is double the usual size (in

TABLE 6.1

Race Differences in Democratic Party Identification, 1974 vs. 1994[a]

Race	Percentages		Odds[b]	
	1974	1994	1974	1994
White	14.71	10.48	.1725	.1171
Black	33.53	40.97	.5044	.6941
Percentage difference				
(white – black)	–18.82	–30.49		
Odds ratio (white/black)	.342	.169		
1974-1994 change in race difference:				
based on percentages: –30.49 – (–18.82) = –11.67%				
based on odds: .169/.342 = .494				

a. Self-identification as "strong Democrat." Sample size is 5,581 (2,806 for 1973/1974 and 2,775 for 1994). Sample consists of all respondents with nonmissing data on race, party identification, and four variables added later as covariates: education, region, gender, and age.
b. "Odds" is defined as $p/(1 - p)$, where p is probability. Because p is percentage/100, odds are calculated here from the percentages: odds = percentage/(100 – percentage).

1994, the GSS switched to a biennial design), I combined the 1973 and 1974 surveys. For convenience, I refer to the combined 1973-1974 surveys simply as 1974.

To facilitate comparison with logistic regression results, Table 6.1 also reports odds of Democratic Party identification. The odds reported in Table 6.1 are calculated from the percentages: odds = percentage/(100 – percentage). In 1974, for example, 14.71% of white respondents identified themselves as strong Democrats—an odds of .1725 (14.71/[100 – 14.71] = .1725).

The results in Table 6.1 suggest that the race gap in Democratic Party identification indeed has increased from 1974 to 1994. In 1974, the white "deficit" in Democratic Party identification stood at 18.82%: 14.71% of whites identified as strong Democrats, as opposed to 33.53% of blacks so identified. In 1994, the deficit had ballooned to 30.49%: 10.48% of whites identified as strong Democrats versus 40.97% of blacks.

In terms of odds, the odds that a white person is identified as a strong Democrat declined from .1725 in 1974 to .1171 in 1994, whereas the odds for an African American increased from .5044 in 1974 to .6941 in 1994. The white/black *odds ratio*—the ratio of the odds that a white person is a strong Democrat to the odds that a black person is a strong Democrat—declined from .342 (.1725/.5044) in 1974 to .169 (.1171/.6941) in 1994. Put another way, being white (as opposed to black) multiplied the odds of being a strong Democrat by .342 in 1974 and by .169 in 1994. In 1974, therefore, the likelihood of being a strong Democrat was substantially less among whites than among blacks, and by 1994 that race difference was even more pronounced.

Observe that the white/black ratio of the odds of being a strong Democrat declined from .342 to .169. The race effect was greater in 1994 than it was 20 years earlier: Being white *in 1994* (as opposed to 1974) multiplies the odds of being a strong Democrat by .494 (Table 6.1). Because whites in 1974 already were less likely than blacks to be strong Democrats, reducing the odds ratio by one half further inflates the race gap in Democratic Party identification.

The next step is to determine the statistical significance of the race differences reported in Table 6.1. Although there are various ways to determine statistical significance here, the most instructive is logistic regression with Democratic Party identification as the dependent variable. By using logistic regression to test race effects for statistical significance, it is an easy next step to add covariates to estimate the effect of race net of the effects of other explanatory variables.

Table 6.2 gives the results of a logistic regression analysis. The term "gross effects" is used in the table's title to emphasize the absence of control variables; the model simply reproduces the raw differences reported in Table 6.1. The model is a changing-parameter model: The interaction term, race times 1994, allows for the race gap in Democratic Party identification to change between 1974 and 1994. The model can be written out as follows:

$$E(Dem) = \alpha + \gamma D_{94} + \beta Race + \delta Race \times D_{94} \qquad (6.7)$$

where *Race* is a dummy variable (1 = white). Note that the racial differences model here and the regional differences model discussed earlier (Equation 6.5) are equivalent in form. Both consist of only four parameters: an intercept (α) and three differences in intercepts (γ, β, and δ). Models of this sort are the simplest form of changing-parameter models.

Table 6.2 reports estimates of the four parameters. Because readers may have more experience working with percentages than with odds, Table 6.2 first reports the results for an ordinary least squares (OLS) regression analysis that parallels the logistic regression analysis. Whereas logistic regression reproduces the odds reported in Table 6.1, OLS reproduces the percentages in Table 6.1. I begin with the OLS results to fix basic principles. It is important to stress that this exercise is for didactic purposes, to

50

TABLE 6.2

Race Differences in Democratic Party Identification,[a] 1974 vs. 1994:
Regression Results for a Changing-Parameter Model of Gross Effects
($N = 5,581$)

Independent Variable	OLS Regression[b]		Logistic Regression[c]		
	Coefficient	p	Logit	Odds Ratio	p
1994 dummy	7.4*	.006	.319*	1.376	.04
Race (1 = white)	−18.8*	< .0001	−1.074*	.342	< .0001
Race × 1994 dummy	−11.7*	< .0001	−.706*	.494	< .0001
Intercept[d]	33.5*	< .0001	−.6841*	.5045	< .0001

a. Self-identification as "strong Democrat."
b. The coefficients reported in the OLS regression can be used to reproduce the percentages in Table 6.1.
The coefficients can be obtained by regressing the dichotomous dummy variable (1 = strong Democrat, 0
otherwise) on the dummies for 1994, race, and race × 1994, and then multiplying the obtained coefficients
by 100; alternatively, to avoid the need to multiply the coefficients by 100, the dependent variable can be
coded (0, 100) instead of (0, 1).
c. The odds ratio is calculated here by taking the antilogarithm (base e) of the logit. The odds ratios above
can be used to reproduce the odds reported in Table 6.1 (see text for elaboration).
d. Coefficient (percentage or logit) for the reference group, that is, for blacks in 1974.
*$p < .05$.

demonstrate how least squares estimation of a gross-effects model reproduces the raw percentages of Table 6.1. The exercise should not be con-
strued as an endorsement of OLS estimation of models with dichotomous
dependent variables. In such models, logistic regression is a more appropriate method for estimating statistical significance. Table 6.2 reports OLS
estimates of significance only so that they can be compared with the
logistic regression estimates.

The Table 6.1 percentages can be reproduced from the OLS estimates by
substitution of the appropriate values for the dummy variables. For blacks
in 1974 we have

$$E(Dem) = \alpha + \gamma D_{94} + \beta Race + \delta D_{94} Race$$

$$= 33.5 + 7.4(0) - 18.8(0) - 11.7(0)$$

$$= 33.5. \tag{6.8}$$

For blacks in 1994, the final two terms again drop out, and $E(Dem) = \alpha +
\gamma D_{94} = 33.5 + 7.4 = 40.9$. For whites in 1974, $Race = 1$ and $D_{94} = 0$, so
$E(Dem) = \alpha + \beta Race = 33.5 - 18.8 = 14.7$. For whites in 1994, $Race = 1$

and $D_{94} = 1$, so $E(Dem) = \alpha + \gamma D_{94} + \beta Race + \delta D_{94}Race = 33.5 + 7.4 - 18.8 - 11.7 = 10.4$.

This exercise illustrates a well-known principle of OLS regression: When all regressors are dummy variables, least squares regression predicts the mean value for each of the categories modeled by the dummy variables. In the special case in which the dependent variable is a dichotomy coded (0, 100), the regression coefficients can be used to recover the actual category percentages. (This follows because a percentage is the mean for a variable coded [0, 100]. For example, if two respondents out of five are strong Democrats, then the mean is $[100 + 100 + 0 + 0 + 0]/5 = 40 =$ the percentage of strong Democrats.)

In a parallel manner, the results from logistic regression with dummy regressors can be used to recover category *odds*. First, consider the intercept. The intercept is the mean value for the reference group (blacks in 1974). In the case of OLS, the intercept is the percentage of blacks in 1974 who identified themselves as strong Democrats (Equation 6.8). In the case of logistic regression, the intercept is the *odds* that an African American in 1974 will be a strong Democrat. Because 33.5% of blacks in 1974 were strong Democrats, the odds is $33.5/(100 - 33.5) = .504$, as given by the intercept in Table 6.2 (within rounding error).

Now consider the odds that an African American is a strong Democrat in 1994. From Table 6.1, we know those odds has increased from .504 to .694. We can also determine from Table 6.2 that the odds has increased, as follows:

$$\text{logit}(Dem) = \alpha + \gamma D_{94} + \beta Race + \delta Race \times D_{94}$$

$$= -.684 + .319 D_{94} - 1.074 Race - .706 Race \times D_{94}$$

$$= -.684 + .319(1) - 1.074(0) - .706(0)$$

$$= -.365. \tag{6.9}$$

The value $-.365$ is the logit (log of the odds) that an African American in 1994 will be a strong Democrat. To convert logits to odds, we take the antilogarithm (to the base e) of $-.365$: logit $= -.365$ implies odds $= e^{-.365}$ $= .694$.

In Equation 6.9, we added the exponents (the logits), then took the antilogarithm to get the odds. Alternatively, because $e^{x + y} = e^x e^y$, we can take the antilogs first and multiply (i.e., $e^x e^y$) instead of summing and then taking the antilog ($e^{x + y}$). Thus, from Equation 6.9, the odds of being a strong Democrat is, for African Americans in 1994, $e^{\{-.684 + .319(1)}$ $^{-1.074(0) - .706(0)\}} = e^{-.684}e^{.319}e^0e^0 = (.505)(1.376)(1)(1) = .695$ ($e^0 = 1$ by definition).

Multiplying the antilogs often is the easier method because standard logistic regression programs report the antilogs along with the logits. These antilogs are labeled "odds ratios" in Table 6.2. The odds for a given group is calculated by multiplying the appropriate odds ratios. Note, for example, that the odds ratios in Table 6.2 imply an odds of .695 (.505 × 1.376) for African Americans in 1994. Substantively, for blacks, the odds of being a strong Democrat increased by a factor of 1.376 from 1974 to 1994 (from odds = .505 to odds = .695).

The story is quite different for whites. For them, the odds of being a strong Democrat declined by a factor of (1.376)(.494) = .680 from 1974 to 1994. This follows from the odds ratios reported in Table 6.2:

$$\text{odds for whites in 1974} = (.505)(.342) \tag{6.10}$$

$$\text{odds for whites in 1994} = (.505)(.342)(1.376)(.494). \tag{6.11}$$

Comparing Equations 6.10 and 6.11, it is immediately apparent that the odds in 1994 is the odds in 1974 multiplied by (1.376)(.494), or .680. For whites, then, the odds of being a strong Democrat declined by a factor of .680 from 1974 to 1994, whereas for African Americans the odds of being a strong Democrat increased by a factor of 1.376. Hence, the *ratio of the odds* for whites to blacks is multiplied by .680/1.376 = .494 from 1974 to 1994.

The changing-parameter odds ratio (.494) is statistically significant, indicating that the racial gap in party identification changed from 1974 to 1994. The coefficient of .494 means that the odds that a white is a strong Democrat, *relative to* the odds that a black is a strong Democrat, was multiplied by .494 from 1974 to 1994. Because whites in 1974 were already less likely to be strong Democrats, this halving of the white/black odds has the effect of *increasing* the race difference in the odds of being a strong Democrat. We conclude, then, that the race gap in Democratic Party identification widened between 1974 and 1994, at least with respect to self-identification as a strong Democrat.[11]

What else can we conclude from Table 6.2? First, consider the results for the 1994 dummy. The reference group is blacks in 1974, so a coefficient for the 1994 dummy compares blacks in 1994 with blacks in 1974. The logit is positive and statistically significant, meaning that blacks identified more strongly with the Democratic Party in 1994 than in 1974. In other words, the 7.4 percentage point increase for blacks (Table 6.1) is statistically significant. Next, consider the results for the race dummy. Because the reference group is blacks in 1974, the logit here compares whites to blacks in 1974. The logit is negative and statistically significant, so we conclude that in 1974 whites were less likely than blacks to identify themselves as strong Democrats. In other words, the 18.8 percentage point difference between blacks and whites in 1974 is not likely to be a sampling fluke ($p < .0001$).[12]

The regressions do *not* tell us whether the decline in Democratic Party identification *among whites* is statistically significant. To determine that, we would need to reverse the coding of the race variable (examples are given below).

Race and Education Differences in Democratic Party Identification

I chose the example of widening race differences in party identification purposely to show how odds for each group (whites in 1974, whites in 1994, etc.) can be recovered from logit coefficients in a changing-parameter model with categorical regressors. In a substantive paper on race and party identification, the natural next step would be to add a list of covariates to see whether the widening race gap in identification with the Democratic Party can be explained by those covariates. I postpone that step for the moment to focus on basic principles of changing-parameter models for *continuous* variables. I use the example of education: Net of the race differences just observed, is the relationship between education and Democratic Party identification different in 1994 from that in 1974? To find out, I add education and education times 1994 to the changing-parameter model of gross race differences.

Table 6.3 reports the results. Because we have switched from a model in which all regressors are categorical to a model in which some are not, the intercept can no longer be interpreted as the mean for the reference group. Instead, the intercept is the predicted value for a reference group member with zeroes on the continuous variables. Hence, the model here predicts that the log-odds of being a self-identified strong Democrat is .41 for an African American in 1974 with no education. If the log-odds is .41, the odds is $e^{.41}$, or 1.51, so the probability is $1.51/(1.51 + 1)$, or .60. We also conclude that the .60 probability applies in 1994 as well as in 1974, because

TABLE 6.3

Race and Education Differences in Democratic Party Identification,[a] 1974
vs. 1994: Regression Results for a Changing-Parameter Model (N = 5,581)

Independent Variable	Logit	Odds Ratio	p
1994 dummy	−.14	.87	.67
Race (1 = white)	−.94*	.39	< .0001
Race × 1994 dummy	−.80*	.45	< .0001
Education	−.106*	.90	< .0001
Education × 1994 dummy	.055*	1.06	.03
Intercept	.41*	1.51	.04

a. Self-identification as "strong Democrat."
*p < .05.

the 1994 dummy fails to attain statistical significance in Table 6.3.[13] This
result is contrary to what we found in Table 6.2, in which, for blacks, the
odds of being a strong Democrat was significantly greater in 1994 than it
was in 1974.

Race effects are the same with education in the model; that is, whites are
less likely than blacks to identify themselves as strong Democrats, and the
gap is widening. Education constant, being white (as opposed to African
American) multiplies the odds of being a strong Democrat by .39 in 1974
and by (.39)(.45) = .18 in 1994. These estimates are very similar to the
estimates of the gross race effects of .342 in 1974 and (.342)(.494) = .169
in 1994 (Tables 6.1). Even with the effects of education controlled for, race
differences in Democratic Party identification have widened.

With regard to the effect of education itself, the better educated are less
likely to identify themselves as strong Democrats. In 1974, an additional
year of education multiplies the odds of being a strong Democrat by .90.
The education × 1994 interaction term is statistically significant (p = .03),
indicating that the effect of education is different in 1994. The logit
coefficient for the interaction term is the estimated *difference* in the 1974
and 1994 slopes, so the estimated slope (logit) for 1994 is the slope for
1974 plus the 1994 increment: −.106 + .055 = −.051. Because the antilog
of −.051 is .95, we can say that in this sample an additional year of
education multiplies the odds of being a strong Democrat by .95 in 1994.
(Alternatively, we could have determined that .95 odds ratio by multiplying
the odds ratios for the 1974 education effect [.90] and the 1994 increment
to the education effect [1.06].)

TABLE 6.4

Race and Education Differences in Democratic Party Identification,[a]
1974 vs. 1994: Regression Results for a Changing-Parameter Model
With Reversal of Coding for the Year Dummy ($N = 5,581$)

Independent Variable	Logit	Odds Ratio	p
1974 dummy	.14	1.15	.67
Race (1 = white)	−1.74*	.18	< .0001
Race × 1974 dummy	.80*	2.22	< .0001
Education	−.052*	.95	.007
Education × 1974 dummy	−.055*	.95	.03
Intercept	.27	1.31	.30

a. Self-identification as "strong Democrat."
*$p < .05$.

In sum, from the results reported in Table 6.3, we can conclude that education has an inverse effect on Democratic Party identification in 1974 ($p < .0001$) and that the education effect is weaker in 1994 than in 1974 ($p = .03$). We *cannot* determine from Table 6.3, however, whether or not the education effect is statistically significant in 1994. We can calculate the sample slope for education in 1994 as −.051 in the logits (above), yet we lack a significance test for that logit.

To test that logit for significance, we can reverse the coding of the year dummy and re-estimate the changing-parameter model. When the year dummy is coded 0 for 1994 and 1 for 1974, the logit coefficient for education represents the estimated effect of education in *1994*, not 1974. That is the coefficient we want to test for significance. (For another application of reverse coding to determine statistical significance, see Firebaugh & Beck, 1994, footnote 12.)

Table 6.4 reports the results for the changing-parameter model with the year dummy coded 1 = 1974. Education's effect in 1994 in fact is statistically significant ($p = .007$, Table 6.4). The logit coefficient we obtain is −.052, consistent with calculations from Table 6.3 (−.106 + .055). In 1994, then, an additional year of education multiplies the odds of being a strong Democrat by $e^{-.052}$, or .95.

To repeat, the point of Table 6.4 is to test the statistical significance of education's effect in 1994. Aside from questions of statistical significance, there is no need to estimate the Table 6.4 model, because the logits and odds ratios for the regressors in Table 6.4 can be calculated from the coefficients in Table 6.3. I nevertheless include both tables because readers will find it instructive to compare them. Readers should note, for example, that reversing the coding for year reverses the sign of the logit for all the terms that include year: year itself, race × year, and education × year. Moreover, reversing the year code reverses the referent for the additive race and education effects in the model—the race and education coefficients now refer to the effects of race and education in 1994, not 1974. Thus, for example, the odds ratio for race is now .18 (Table 6.4), which is the odds ratio in 1994, not in 1974.

I include Table 6.4 because it also helps to underscore the point that direct tests for *change* in an effect (as used in the changing-parameter model) are not to be confused with significance tests for the separate effects. Experienced researchers will recognize this situation: In group A, the coefficient for variable X has a p value smaller than .05, so at the $\alpha =$ .05 level, we conclude that X has an effect in group A. In group B, the coefficient is slightly smaller and has a p value larger than .05, so we conclude that X has no effect in group B, yet the *difference* in the two coefficients for X is *not* statistically significant. Conversely, the difference might be statistically significant, even though the separate coefficients are not (this might occur, for example, when one sample coefficient is positive and the other is negative).

The lesson for researchers is to be wary of inferring change in the effect of a variable from change in the statistical significance of the variable's effect. If X has a statistically significant effect at time 1 but not at time 2, we cannot infer that the effect of X has changed significantly. Changing-parameter models provide direct tests for change in a variable's effects, and researchers who want to draw conclusions about *changing effects* should employ such direct tests, because change in the statistical significance of the effect of X is no guarantee of a statistically significant change in the effect of X.

Net Effects of Race on Democratic Party Identification

The logical next step in the analysis of the race gap in party identification is to add covariates to determine whether the race gap—and the widening of that gap—can be accounted for by sociodemographic differences between blacks and whites. For the sake of illustration, I add region, gender, and age (in its quadratic form: age and age^2) to the changing-parameter model reported in Table 6.4. These are the covariates (along with education,

TABLE 6.5

Net Effects of Race and Education on Democratic Party Identification,[a] 1974
vs. 1994: Regression Results for a Changing-Parameter Model ($N = 5,581$)

Independent Variable	Logit	Odds Ratio	p
1994 dummy	−.09	.91	.78
Race (1 = white)	−1.04*	.36	< .0001
Race × 1994 dummy	−.83*	.44	< .0001
Education	−.06*	.94	.0002
Education × 1994 dummy	.04	1.05	.07
Region (1 = South)	.07	1.07	.40
Gender (1 = women)	−.03	.97	.70
Age[b]	.04*	1.04	< .0001
Age-squared[b]	−.0002	1.00	.11
Intercept	−.91*	.40	.0004

a. Self-identification as "strong Democrat."
b. Age is measured as respondent's age minus 16.
*$p < .05$.

which is already in the model) employed in the Hout, Brooks, and Manza
(1995) study of class differences in voting for the Democratic presidential
candidate (more on this study in the next section).

Tables 6.5 and 6.6 report results with the covariates added (Table 6.5
with year coded as $1 = 1994$ and Table 6.6 with year coded as $1 = 1974$).
In brief, the net effects of race are the same as the gross effects. Adding the
covariates scarcely affects the coefficients for race and race × 1994. Race
differences in identification with the Democratic Party in the United States
are not attributable to race differences in education, region, gender, or age.

Second Illustration of Changing-Parameter Model:
Class and Democratic Party Identification

Recent research by Hout, Brooks, and Manza (1995, p. 805) presents
evidence of "a historic realignment in the relationship between class and voting
behavior in U.S. Presidential elections in the postwar period." Specifically,
from NES data they find evidence of polarization in the voting of the middle
class, with support for Democratic candidates increasing among professionals
and technicians and declining among managers and sales workers.

By substituting an appropriate measure of class for the race variable used
in the changing-parameter race model above, we have a ready-made test

58

Net Effects of Race and Education on Democratic Party Identification,[a]
1974 vs. 1994: Regression Results for a Changing-Parameter Model
With Reversal of Coding for the Year Dummy ($N = 5,581$)

Independent Variable	Logit	Odds Ratio	p
1974 dummy	.09	1.09	.78
Race (1 = white)	−1.87*	.16	< .0001
Race × 1974 dummy	.83*	2.29	< .0001
Education	−.02	.98	.40
Education × 1974 dummy	−.04	.96	.07
Region (1 = South)	.07	1.07	.40
Gender (1 = women)	−.03	.97	.70
Age[b]	.04*	1.04	< .0001
Age-squared[b]	−.0002	1.00	.11
Intercept	−1.00*	.37	.0008

a. Self-identification as "strong Democrat."
b. Age is measured as respondent's age minus 16.
*$p < .05$.

for whether the middle-class polarization argument is supported by GSS data on Democratic Party identification. The class and party identification example is especially apt here because it demonstrates the application of the changing-parameter model to the case of multiple-category regressors. Here the issue turns on two categories—professional/technical versus managerial/sales occupations—that are embedded in a class structure encompassing other occupational groups. In the context of a variable with multiple categories, our particular interest lies in changes in the party identification of just two of the categories.

There are two ways to proceed in the case of such "targeted comparisons" in a polytomous variable. One method is to restrict the analysis to the comparison categories of interest. In testing the middle-class polarization thesis, for example, we would analyze only the middle-class sample. The second method is to include the entire sample and pool all other occupations into a residual dummy variable. Thus, all occupations other than managerial, sales, professional, and technical are lumped into an "other occupations" dummy. For didactic purposes, I employ both methods in analyzing the middle-class polarization thesis.

Table 6.7 reports the gross differences in Democratic Party identification for the three occupation categories (managerial/sales, professional/technical,

TABLE 6.7

Class Differences in Democratic Party Identification, 1974 vs. 1994:
Percentages and Odds[a]

	Percentages		Odds	
	1974	1994	1974	1994
Middle class ($n = 1,840$)	10.38	12.54	.116	.143
Managerial and sales	11.35	10.25	.128	.114
Professional and technical	9.44	15.01	.104	.177
OtherOcc ($n = 3,353$)	19.97	15.72	.250	.187

Pertinent odds ratios	
Odds for managers in 1994: odds for managers in 1974	0.891[b]
Odds for professionals: odds for managers (1974)	0.813[b]
Odds for professionals: odds for managers (1994)	1.553
Odds for OtherOcc: odds for managers (1974)	1.953[b]
Odds for OtherOcc: odds for managers (1994)	1.640
Change in effect, professionals:managers[c]	1.91[b]
Change in effect, OtherOcc:managers[d]	0.84[b]

a. Self-identification as "strong Democrat." Sample size is 5,193. Sample consists of respondents with nonmissing data on occupation, party identification, gender, race, age, and region.
b. Ratios appear as coefficients in the logistic regression in Table 6.8.
c. Odds for professionals: odds for managers, 1994 ratio divided by 1974 ratio (1.553/.813).
d. 1.640/1.953.

and "OtherOcc"). The table reports the odds of self-identification as a strong Democrat for each of the groups; the odds in turn were calculated from the percentages reported in the table. From the odds, it is a simple matter to calculate the change in odds for the categories of interest (here, professional/technical versus managerial/sales is shortened to "professionals" versus "managers"). The change in odds can then be compared with the odds ratio for the appropriate changing-parameter term in the logistic regression analysis of the *gross-effects model*. Assuming that variables are coded the same way in both instances, the two estimates should agree (within rounding error). If they do not, the source of the error should be located.

The raw figures appear to lend support to the middle-class polarization thesis. For the middle class as a whole, the odds of being a strong Democrat increased somewhat, from .116 in 1974 to .143 in 1994. That overall increase masks an interesting difference within the middle class: The odds of being a strong Democrat remained constant or declined slightly for managers, whereas the odds increased substantially for professionals. As

TABLE 6.8

Middle-Class Democratic Party Identification,[a] 1974 vs. 1994:
Regression Results for a Changing-Parameter Model of Gross Effects

Independent Variable	Targeted Sample[b] (middle class only)			Entire Sample[c] (all occupations)		
	Logit	Odds Ratio	p	Logit	Odds Ratio	p
1994 dummy	−.11	.89	.60	−.11	.89	.60
Prof dummy	−.21	.81	.39	−.21	.81	.39
Prof × 1994	.64*	1.90	.03	.64*	1.90	.03
OtherOcc dummy[d]	—	—	—	.67*	1.95	< .0001
OtherOcc × 1994	—	—	—	−.18	.84	.45
Intercept	−2.06*	.128	< .0001	−2.06*	.128	< .0001

a. Self-identification as "strong Democrat."
b. $N = 1,840$. Includes professional and technical workers (coded 1 for the Prof dummy) and managerial and sales workers.
c. $N = 5,193$.
d. Includes all workers not classified as professional, technical, managerial, or sales.
*$p < .05$.

a result, the two groups reverse position with regard to the strength of their identification with the Democratic Party. In 1974, managers were more likely to identify themselves as strong Democrats; in 1994, professionals were more likely to so identify themselves.

We do not know, however, whether these sample differences are statistically significant. To determine statistical significance, we turn to the results of logistic regression (Table 6.8). As before, the dependent variable is the log-odds of self-identification as a strong Democrat. In the "targeted comparison" method, the sample is restricted to the managerial and professional occupational categories. In this case, the sample size is 1,840, and there are three regressors: a dummy variable for 1994, a dummy variable for occupation ("Prof") coded 1 for professionals and technicians and 0 for managers and sales workers, and the changing-parameter term, Prof × 1994. In the unrestricted approach, all occupations are included, so the sample is larger ($N = 5,193$), and two regressors must be added: an "OtherOcc" dummy (coded 1 for occupations other than managerial and professional), and a changing-parameter term, OtherOcc × 1994.

The results support the middle-class polarization thesis. The changing-parameter term, Prof × 1994, is the key here. The odds ratio for Prof × 1994 is 1.90 ($p = .03$, Table 6.8). In other words, the ratio of the odds of being a strong Democrat for professionals relative to managers changed by a factor of 1.90 from 1974 to 1994. Checking Table 6.7 verifies that figure: The odds ratio, professionals to managers, is .813 in 1974 and 1.553 in 1994, so from 1974 to 1994 the professionals-to-managers ratio is multiplied by 1.553/.813, or 1.91 (with rounding error).

Table 6.8 also indicates that in 1974 there was no difference between professionals and managers in Democratic Party identification. The 1974 difference between professionals and managers is reflected in the coefficient for the Prof dummy: The odds ratio is .81, which is not statistically significant. *Change* in that odds ratio is statistically significant (the Prof × 1994 term). As explained earlier, it does not automatically follow that the *1994 difference* between professionals and managers is statistically significant, so I tested the 1994 difference by reversing the coding of the year dummy (not shown). That difference in fact is significant in this sample (odds ratio = 1.55, p = .02).

The restricted and unrestricted samples give the same results here. The equivalence is not a fluke. Although the restricted sample uses a subsample of the data used in the other method, both methods fit the same odds; that is, both fit the odds of Democratic Party identification for professionals and managers in 1974 and 1994. In other words, both methods are designed to reproduce (within rounding error) the pertinent odds in Table 6.7, so they give the same results.

Why use the entire sample if the targeted sample gives the same results? There are two reasons. First, the entire sample gives information on trends in Democratic Party identification outside the middle class, so we can place the findings about middle-class polarization in a broader context. Recall that Prof × 1994 examines 1974-1994 change in the odds of Democratic Party identification for professionals relative to managers. Likewise, OtherOcc × 1994 examines change in the same odds ratio, but for *all other workers* (non-middle class) relative to managers; for non-middle-class workers relative to managers, the change in the odds ratio is not statistically significant (p = .45). Relative to managers, then, professionals have shifted toward the Democratic Party, yet this shift appears *not* to be part of a general shift toward the Democratic Party—something we would not have known had the analysis been restricted to professionals and managers.

Second, using the entire sample generally leads to better estimates of net effects. As demonstrated in Table 6.8, both methods give the same results for gross effects, because both methods replicate the odds ratios in Table 6.7. Results for the two methods generally differ when control variables are added, however, because estimates of the effects of control variables generally will not be the same for the two samples.

TABLE 6.9

Middle-Class Democratic Party Identification,[a] 1974 vs. 1994: Regression Results for a Changing-Parameter Model With a Continuous Regressor

Independent Variable	Targeted Sample[b] (middle class only)			Entire Sample[c] (all occupations)		
	Logit	Odds Ratio	p	Logit	Odds Ratio	p
1994 dummy	−.16	.85	.06	−.02	.98	.93
Prof dummy	−.36	.70	.06	.02	1.02	.94
Prof × 1994	.74*	2.10	.002	.60*	1.81	.049
OtherOcc dummy[d]	—	—	—	.49*	1.63	.005
OtherOcc × 1994	—	—	—	−.15	.86	.51
Education	−.10*	.90	< .0001	−.09*	.91	< .0001
Intercept	−.38*	.681	.013	−.92*	.40	< .0001

a. Self-identification as "strong Democrat."
b. $N = 1,840$. Includes professional and technical workers (coded 1 for the Prof dummy) and managerial and sales workers.
c. $N = 5,193$.
d. Includes all workers not classified as professional, technical, managerial, or sales.
*$p < .05$.

To illustrate, I added education to the middle-class polarization model (see Table 6.9). In examining Table 6.9, remember that the estimate of education's effect is based on middle-class respondents in the first regression and on the entire sample in the second regression. It would be highly unusual for the education slope to be exactly the same for both samples; when the estimated effect of education differs, we expect the estimated effect of the other explanatory variables to differ as well (as they do here), because those other variables are related to education.

Summary and Extensions

Chapter 6 has presented a model designed to detect changes in the effects of explanatory variables in repeated surveys. The model's defining feature is interaction terms having the form X times D_{YR}, where X is an explanatory variable (categorical or continuous) and D_{YR} is a dummy variable for survey. The model is simple yet flexible. Illustrations from the General Social Surveys were presented in some detail to demonstrate the model's flexibility as well as to address practical problems that arise in the model's use.

It is important to note that this model is intended to document change, not to explain it. Further analysis—or a different model— is needed to explain observed change. One promising strategy is to express individual-level parameters as functions of macrolevel characteristics that vary over time (DiPrete & Grusky, 1990; Firebaugh & Haynie, in press). This strategy mimics the multilevel approach used in the study of school effects (e.g., Bryk & Raudenbush, 1992), except that the context is *time*, not school.

The multilevel approach to studying changing effects over time begins, then, by modeling individual-level parameters themselves as functions of macro variables and a disturbance term. Because of the disturbance term in the macro equations, the multilevel model is a random-effects model, and ordinary least squares is not appropriate. The interaction model described earlier is a fixed-effects model, so (depending on the nature of the dependent variable) it can be estimated using OLS or logistic regression. The multilevel model, in contrast, requires estimation methods that are beyond the scope of this book (DiPrete & Grusky, 1990).

7. SUMMARY:
ANALYZING SOCIAL CHANGE

As noted in the preface, I could have titled this book *How to Use Repeated Surveys to Analyze Social Change*. The core of the book consists of explanations of four methods for studying social change. The methods differ because they ask different questions about change.

The first method is trend analysis. Trend analysis asks whether the average value of Y is changing over time for some group; hence, in trend analysis, $E(Y)$ is expressed *as a function of time*. Because these are trends for groups, not individuals, the trend analysis described here is macrolevel. (Trend analysis for individuals would require panel data.) Very often, interest centers on whether trends are converging or diverging for different groups. Chapter 3 described and illustrated how that issue can be explored.

The second method is proximate decomposition of trends. Here, the focus is on the proximate source of social change: How much is due to net change among individuals, and how much is due to population turnover? Chapter 4 described two decomposition methods—one based on linear regression, the other on algebra.

The third method is decomposition of change in one variable in terms of change in the *levels* and *effects* of other variables. Chapter 5 described a general model for decomposing aggregate change along those lines. The change-decomposition model is based on the decomposition equation of regression standardization but applies it to the decomposition of change, as opposed to the decomposition of group differences.

The fourth method focuses on change in the effects of variables at the individual level. Chapter 6 described a model—the changing-parameter model—for determining the time-dependence of individual-level relationships. The changing-parameter model bears a superficial resemblance to the convergence/divergence model for trends (Chapter 3), because both models are built around interaction terms involving time, but the similarity ends there. Because trends are changes in the expected value of Y as time changes, time is treated as continuous in trend analysis, and $E(Y)$ is expressed as a function of time. The changing-parameter model, in contrast, treats $E(Y)$ as a function of Xs at a discrete point in time, where the *effect* of the Xs on $E(Y)$ is a function of time.

Because time per se is not a causal variable, trend analysis is descriptive. Moreover, trend analyses typically employ a limited number of variables. The trend analysis reported in Table 3.1, for example, employed only three variables (but used all the General Social Surveys from 1973 to 1993). In the simplest case, trend analysis is bivariate: a variable Y and time. Very often, though, the purpose of trend analysis is to determine whether trends differ for population subgroups. In that case, there are at least three variables: Y, time, and a variable encompassing the subgroups. In some cases, the subgroups reflect classification across the categories of several variables. For example, Firebaugh and Harley (1995) examine trends in job satisfaction by race-gender groups (white men, white women, and so on). Trends are rarely examined for groups cross-classified along more than two or three dimensions, because that would lead to a proliferation of trends to examine and a concomitant reduction in the sample size for each trend. Trend models therefore tend to be fairly simple.

Although trend analysis requires only a few variables, it requires several measurements of those variables. Multiple measurement is a key point here. Change-decomposition and changing-parameter analyses require only two points in time (but generally employ a much longer list of variables), so surveys that have been repeated only once or twice are possible candidates for the change-decomposition and changing-parameter models described here but are not candidates for serious trend analysis. With regard to proximate decomposition, cohort replacement effects are best estimated with multiple measurement—in such a case, the linear decomposition method often can be used—yet it is feasible to estimate cohort replacement's contribution to change between two surveys (as in several examples above). Otherwise, the data demands for proximate decomposition are not onerous. Separating the contributions of cohort replacement from those of individual change necessitates the measurement of only three variables: a dependent variable, birth year, and survey year.

The four methods—trend analysis, proximate decomposition, change-decomposition, and changing-parameter models—are designed to exploit the repetition in repeated surveys. These methods offer simple but useful tools for studying social change. Ultimately, the worth of a tool is proven in use, and the value of these methods for studying social change will be realized only as social scientists use them.

NOTES

1. One virtue of repeated surveys is that they can be pooled to get a sufficient sample size to permit the study of some population subgroups that might otherwise be hard to study. Using the GSS, for example, one could study Catholics, or divorcees, or even divorced Catholics. Because of the need to accumulate the cases over time, however, such studies generally must assume that effects are constant over time.

2. In some instances, cohort differences might arise from their relative *size*. Members of a relatively small cohort, for example, might benefit from smaller classes in school and from less competition when entering the job market, whereas the opposite is true for larger cohorts. We do not focus on this type of cohort effect because—in contrast to other types of cohort effects—size-based cohort effects are not hard to distinguish empirically from age and period effects. Cohort size simply can be entered as a variable in a model with a measure of age and period. Other types of cohort effects are much harder to separate from age and period effects (see below).

3. Weighting by the variable *OVERSAMP* in GSS reweights the sample to adjust for the oversampling of blacks in 1982 and 1987.

4. Because these estimates assume a linear trend, they generally vary from the estimate based on the mean of the initial survey itself.

5. It is important not to equate the cross-cohort slope, β_2, with a cohort *effect*, because (to repeat) β_2 could reflect age effects as well as cohort effects.

6. See Firebaugh (1992) for a discussion of why algebraic decomposition might overstate cohort replacement effects for wide decomposition intervals. As discussed in that article, algebraic decomposition works best for closely spaced surveys. It also should be noted that further partitioning of the cohort replacement component (e.g., into the part resulting from entering and exiting cohorts versus the part resulting from differential mortality among spanning cohorts) is not straightforward.

7. The GSS samples households, not individuals, so single adults are oversampled. Because marital status might be related to gender role attitudes, I weighted the GSS data using Current Population Survey figures for marital status.

8. All items are coded 0 or 1, with 0 = traditional response, so an increase in the mean indicates an erosion of support for traditional attitudes. It is unlikely that the erosion stems largely from changes in perceptions regarding socially desirable responses. As explained below, the erosion occurs in large part because cohorts differ in their gender role attitudes, and it is unlikely that cohorts are differentially susceptible to the effects of social desirability.

9. "Change for surviving adults, 1972-1988" refers to change among those born during 1899-1954, because respondents in GSS range in age from 18 to 89. To estimate change for the average survivor, then, one might be tempted to separate out those cohorts as a group and simply subtract the 1972 overall mean from the 1988 overall mean. This shortcut will not do for estimating the average change among *survivors*, however, because it uses the cohort shares (p_j) for 1972, not 1988, to calculate the 1972 mean for survivors.

Obviously, unless older and younger cohorts have the same mortality rates, the p_j for 1972 will differ from those for 1988.

10. Teixeira (1987, p. 77) notes that coefficients for the time dummies (i.e., the intercepts) become "uninterpretable" when he adds changing-parameter terms in his analysis, so he reports results only for his additive decompositions. Uninterpretable intercepts are symptomatic of the origin-dependence problem described earlier, and origin-dependence is the likely culprit in Teixeira's changing-parameter analysis.

11. Abramson and colleagues (1994, Tables 8-2 and 8-3) report 1952-1992 NES data on party identification for blacks and whites separately. It is interesting that the NES data for 1974 and 1992 fail to indicate a widening race gap using "strong Democrat" as the criterion: Change in "percent strong Democrat" is virtually zero for both whites and blacks, 1974 versus 1992. Reconciling the GSS and NES data on this point is beyond the scope of the analysis presented here. I analyze the race gap in the GSS data and leave the question of race gaps in the NES data to others.

12. Remember that the coefficients reported in Table 6.2 are based on regressors that are dummy coded. The point is worth stressing because logit analyses often employ effect coding, not dummy coding, for categorical variables. For example, instead of coding race as 1 for whites and 0 for blacks, race could be coded as 1 for whites and –1 for blacks. Effect coding would yield identical results, but the results would appear to be different because of the different values assigned to the regressors. For dichotomies (as in Table 6.2), doubling effect-coded logits converts them to the logits given by dummy coding.

13. The sample logit for the 1994 dummy is –.14 in Table 6.3. The null hypothesis is that the population logit is zero. When the logit is zero, the odds ratio is 1 (because by definition $e^0 = 1$). An equivalent null hypothesis, therefore, is that the odds ratio is 1. Obviously, an odds ratio of 1 means there is no effect, because multiplication by 1 has no effect. For the model in Table 6.3, for example, the estimated odds that an African American in 1994 with no years of education will be a self-identified strong Democrat is 1.51 (the odds in 1974) *times* the odds ratio for the 1994 dummy. Because we fail to reject the null hypothesis that the odds ratio for 1994 is 1, we have 1.51(1) = 1.51.

REFERENCES

ABRAMSON, P., and ALDRICH, J. H. (1982) "The decline of electoral participation in America." *American Political Science Review* 76:502-521.

ABRAMSON, P., ALDRICH, J. H., and ROHDE, D. W. (1994) *Change and Continuity in the 1992 Elections*. Washington, DC: Congressional Quarterly.

AGRESTI, A., and FINLAY, B. (1986) *Statistical Methods for the Social Sciences* (2nd ed.). San Francisco: Dellen.

ALEXANDER, J. C., GEISEN, B., MUNCH, R., and SMELSER, N. J. (Eds.) (1987) *The Macro-Micro Link*. Berkeley: University of California Press.

BENNETT, S., and BENNETT, L. (1987) "Political participation." *Annual Review of Political Science* 2:157-204.

BRODY, R. A. (1978) "The puzzle of political participation in America." In A. King (Ed.), *The New American Political System* (pp. 287-324). Washington, DC: American Enterprise Institute.

BRYK, A. S., and RAUDENBUSH, S. W. (1992) *Hierarchical Linear Models: Applications and Data Analysis Methods*. Newbury Park, CA: Sage.

CAMPBELL, A., CONVERSE, P., MILLER, W., and STOKES, D. (1960) *The American Voter*. New York: Wiley.

CLOGG, C. C., and ELIASON, S. R. (1986) "On regression standardization for moments." *Sociological Methods and Research* 14:423-446.

COLEMAN, J. S. (1986) "Social theory, social research, and a theory of action." *American Journal of Sociology* 91:1309-1335.

COMTE, A. (1974) *The Positive Philosophy, Book VI: Social Physics* (Translated by Harriet Martineau). New York: AMS. (Original work published 1839)

DAS GUPTA, P. (1978) "A general method of decomposing a difference between two rates into several components." *Demography* 15:99-112.

DAS GUPTA, P. (1993) *Standardization and Decomposition of Rates: A User's Manual*. Washington, DC: Government Printing Office.

DAVIS, J. A. (1992) "Changeable weather in a cooling climate atop the liberal plateau: Conversion and replacement in forty-two General Social Survey items, 1972-1989." *Public Opinion Quarterly* 56:261-306.

DAVIS, J. A., and SMITH, T. W. (1992) *The NORC General Social Survey*. Newbury Park, CA: Sage.

DAVIS, J. A., and SMITH, T. W. (1994) *General Social Surveys, 1972-1994 [MRDF]* (NORC ed.). Chicago: NORC.

DAY, C. L. (1990) *What Older Americans Think*. Princeton, NJ: Princeton University Press.

DiPRETE, T. A., and GRUSKY, D. B. (1990) "The multilevel analysis of trends with repeated cross-sectional data." In C. C. Clogg (Ed.), *Sociological Methodology 1990* (pp. 337-368). Oxford, UK: Basil Blackwell.

DONZA, M., DUNCAN, G. J., CORCORAN, M., and GROSKIND, F. (1988) "The guns of autumn? Age differences in support for income transfers to the young and the old." *Public Opinion Quarterly* 52:441-466.

DUNCAN, G., and KALTON, G. (1987) "Issues of design and analysis of surveys across time." *International Statistical Review* 55:97-117.

DURKHEIM, E. (1938) *The Rules of Sociological Method.* Glencoe, IL: Free Press. (Original work published 1895)

EASTERLIN, R. (1980) *Birth and Fortune: The Impact of Numbers on Personal Welfare.* New York: Basic Books.

ELDER, G. H., JR. (1974) *Children of the Great Depression.* Chicago: University of Chicago Press.

FINKEL, S. E. (1995) *Causal Analysis With Panel Data.* Sage University Paper series on Quantitative Applications in the Social Sciences, 07-105. Thousand Oaks, CA: Sage.

FIREBAUGH, G. (1989) "Methods for estimating cohort replacement effects." In C. C. Clogg (Ed.), *Sociological Methodology 1989* (pp. 243-262). Oxford, UK: Basil Blackwell.

FIREBAUGH, G. (1990) "Replacement effects, cohort and otherwise: Response to Rodgers." In C. C. Clogg (Ed.), *Sociological Methodology 1990* (pp. 439-446). Oxford, UK: Basil Blackwell.

FIREBAUGH, G. (1992) "Where does social change come from? Estimating the relative contributions of individual change and population turnover." *Population Research and Policy Review* 11:1-20.

FIREBAUGH, G., and BECK, F. D. (1994) "Does economic growth benefit the masses? Growth, dependence, and welfare in the Third World." *American Sociological Review* 59:631-653.

FIREBAUGH, G., and CHEN, K. (1995) "Vote turnout of Nineteenth Amendment women: The enduring effect of disenfranchisement." *American Journal of Sociology* 100:972-996.

FIREBAUGH, G., and DAVIS, K. E. (1988) "Trends in antiblack prejudice 1972-1984: Region and cohort effects." *American Journal of Sociology* 94:251-272.

FIREBAUGH, G., and HARLEY, B. (1991) "Trends in U.S. church attendance: Secularization and revival, or merely life-cycle effects?" *Journal for the Scientific Study of Religion* 30:487-500.

FIREBAUGH, G., and HARLEY, B. (1995) "Trends in job satisfaction in the United States by race, gender, and type of occupation." In R. L. Simpson and I. H. Simpson (Eds.), *Research in the Sociology of Work, Vol. 5: The Meaning of Work* (pp. 87-104). Greenwich, CT: JAI.

FIREBAUGH, G., and HAYNIE, D. L. (in press) "Using repeated surveys to study aging and social change." In M. A. Hardy (Ed.), *Conceptual and Methodological Issues in the Study of Aging and Social Change.* Thousand Oaks, CA: Sage.

FOX, M. F., and FIREBAUGH, G. (1992) "Confidence in science: The gender gap." *Social Science Quarterly* 73:101-113.

GALLUP, G., and NEWPORT, F. (1991) "For first time, more Americans approve of interracial marriage than disapprove." *Gallup Poll Monthly* (August):60-61.

GLENN, N. (1976) "Cohort analysts' futile quest: Statistical attempts to separate age, period, and cohort effects." *American Sociological Review* 41:900-904.

GLENN, N. (1977) *Cohort Analysis.* Sage University Papers series on Quantitative Applications in the Social Sciences, 07-005. Beverly Hills, CA: Sage.

GLENN, N. (1980) "Values, attitudes, and beliefs." In O. G. Brim, Jr., and J. Kagan (Eds.), *Constancy and Change in Human Development* (pp. 596-640). Cambridge, MA: Harvard University Press.

70

HAGENAARS, J. A. (1990) *Categorical Longitudinal Analysis: Loglinear Panel, Trends, and Cohort Analysis*. Newbury Park, CA: Sage.
HOUT, M., BROOKS, C., and MANZA, J. (1995, December) "The Democratic class struggle in the United States, 1948-1992." *American Sociological Review* 60:805-828.
JOHNSTON, D. F. (Ed.) (1981) *Measurement of Subjective Phenomena*. Washington, DC: Government Printing Office.
JONES, F. L., and KELLEY, J. (1984) "Decomposing differences between groups: A cautionary note on measuring discrimination." *Sociological Methods and Research* 12:323-343.
KALTON, G. (1983) *Introduction to Survey Sampling*. Sage University Papers series on Quantitative Applications in the Social Sciences, 07-035. Beverly Hills, CA: Sage.
KENDALL, M. G. (1973) *Time-Series*. New York: Hafner Press.
KIECOLT, K. J., and NATHAN, L. E. (1985) *Secondary Analysis of Survey Data*. Sage University Paper series on Quantitative Applications in the Social Sciences, 07-053. Beverly Hills, CA: Sage.
KISH, L. (1983) "Data collection for details over space and time." In T. Wright (Ed.), *Statistical Methods and the Improvement of Data Quality* (pp. 73-84). New York: Academic Press.
KISH, L. (1986) "Timing of surveys for public policy." *Australian Journal of Statistics* 28:1-12.
KITAGAWA, E. (1955) "Components of a difference between two rates." *Journal of the American Statistical Association* 30:1168-1194.
KLEPPNER, P. (1982) *Who Voted? The Dynamics of Electoral Turnout, 1870-1980*. New York: Praeger.
KOTLIKOFF, L. J. (1992) *Generational Accounting*. New York: Free Press.
LESTHAEGE, R., and SURKYN, J. (1988) "Cultural dynamics and economic theories of fertility change." *Population and Development Review* 14:1-45.
LONG, J. S., and MIETHE, T. D. (1988) "The statistical comparison of groups." In J. Scott Long (Ed.), *Common Problems/Proper Solutions* (pp. 108-131). Newbury Park, CA: Sage.
LONGMAN, P. (1987) *Born to Pay: The New Politics of Aging in the United States*. Boston: Houghton Mifflin.
MANNHEIM, K. (1952) "The problem of generations." In *Essays on the Sociology of Knowledge* (pp. 276-322). London: Routledge and Kegan Paul. (Original work published 1927)
MARKUS, G. (1979) *Analyzing Panel Data*. Sage University Paper series on Quantitative Applications in the Social Sciences, 07-018. Beverly Hills, CA: Sage.
MASON, K. O., MASON, W. M., WINSBOROUGH, H. H., and POOLE, K. W. (1973) "Some methodological issues in cohort analysis of archival data." *American Sociological Review* 38:242-258.
MENARD, S. (1991) *Longitudinal Research*. Sage University Paper series on Quantitative Applications in the Social Sciences, 07-076. Newbury Park, CA: Sage.
MERRIAM, C. E., and GOSNELL, H. F. (1924) *Non-Voting: Causes and Methods of Control*. Chicago: University of Chicago Press.
NORPOTH, H. (1987) "Under way and here to stay: Party realignment in the 1980s?" *Public Opinion Quarterly* 51:376-391.
PASET, P. S., and TAYLOR, R. D. (1991) "Black and white women's attitudes toward interracial marriage." *Psychological Reports* 69:753-754.

71

RASINSKI, K. A. (1988) "The effect of question wording on public support for government spending." Chicago: NORC.

RODGERS, W. (1990) "Interpreting the components of time trends." In C. C. Clogg (Ed.), *Sociological Methodology 1990* (pp. 421-438). Oxford, UK: Basil Blackwell.

ROSENBAUM, W. A., and BUTTON, J. W. (1992) "Perceptions of intergenerational conflict: The politics of young vs. old in Florida." *Journal of Aging Studies* 6:385-396.

RYDER, N. B. (1965) "The cohort as a concept in the study of social change." *American Sociological Review* 30:843-861.

SAYRS, L. W. (1989) *Pooled Time Series Analysis*. Sage University Paper series on Quantitative Applications in the Social Sciences, 07-070. Newbury Park, CA: Sage.

SMITH, H. L., MORGAN, S. P., and KOROPECKYJ-COX, T. (1996) "A decomposition of trends in the nonmarital fertility ratios of blacks and whites in the United States, 1960-1992." *Demography* 33:141-151.

SMITH, T. W. (1987) "That which we call welfare by any other name would smell sweeter: An analysis of the impact of question wording on response patterns." *Public Opinion Quarterly* 51:75-83.

SMITH, T. W. (1988) *Timely Artifacts: A Review of Measurement Variation in the 1972-1988 GSS Data* (Methodological Report No. 56). Chicago: NORC.

SMITH, T. W. (1992) "Some thoughts on the nature of context effects." In N. Schwarz and S. Sudman (Eds.), *Context Effects in Social and Psychological Research* (pp. 163-184). New York: Springer-Verlag.

SMITH, T. W. (1993) *Is there real opinion change?* (Social Change Report No. 36). Chicago: NORC.

SMITH, T. W., ARNOLD, B. J., and WESELY, J. K. (1995) *Annotated Bibliography of Papers Using the General Social Surveys* (10th ed.). Ann Arbor, MI: Inter-University Consortium for Political and Social Research.

SOBEL, M. E. (1983) "Some large-sample standard errors for components of a mean difference under a linear model." In S. Leinhardt (Ed.), *Sociological Methodology 1983-1984* (pp. 169-193). San Francisco: Jossey-Bass.

STEPHENSON, C. B. (1978) *Weighting the General Social Surveys for Bias Relating to Household Size* (Methodological Report No. 3). Chicago: NORC.

TEIXEIRA, R. A. (1987) *Why Americans Don't Vote: Turnout Decline in the United States 1960-1984*. New York: Greenwood.

TEIXEIRA, R. A. (1992) *The Disappearing American Voter*. Washington, DC: Brookings Institution.

VERBA, S., and NIE, N. (1972) *Participation in America*. New York: Harper & Row.

VINOVSKIS, M. A. (1993) "An historical perspective on support for schooling by different age cohorts." In V. Bengtson and W. A. Achenbaum (Eds.), *The Changing Contract Across Generations* (pp. 45-64). Hawthorne, NY: Aldine de Gruyter.

WILMOTH, J. R. (1990) "Variation in vital rates by age, period, and cohort." In C. C. Clogg (Ed.), *Sociological Methodology 1990* (pp. 295-336). Oxford, UK: Basil Blackwell.

WOLFINGER, R. E., and ROSENSTONE, S. J. (1980) *Who Votes?* New Haven, CT: Yale University Press.

ABOUT THE AUTHOR

GLENN FIREBAUGH (Ph.D., Indiana University-Bloomington) is Professor of Sociology at Pennsylvania State University and Senior Scientist at the university's Population Research Institute. He uses repeated survey data to study the demographic roots of social change in the United States, and aggregate cross-national data to study the determinants of mass welfare in the Third World. At present, he is developing methods for decomposing change in inequality and is applying those methods to decompose change in income inequality across countries. He also serves as Editor of the *American Sociological Review*.